THE
TORCH
LIGHTERS
REVISITED

THE
TORCH LIGHTERS
REVISITED

COLEMAN MORRISON.
Temple University
and
MARY C. AUSTIN
University of Hawaii

Funded in part by a grant from Temple University

INTERNATIONAL READING ASSOCIATION
800 Barksdale Road   Newark, Delaware 19711

Copyright 1977 by the
International Reading Association, Inc.
Library of Congress Cataloging in Publication Data
Morrison, Coleman.
     The torch lighters revisited.
     Bibliography: p.
     1. Reading, Teachers of.   I. Austin, Mary C., joint
author.   II. Title.
LB1050.M585   428'.4'07   76-56776
ISBN 0-87207-933-3

Contents

The International Reading Association attempts, through its publications, to provide a forum for a wide spectrum of opinion on reading. This policy permits divergen viewpoints without assuming the endorsement of the Association.

Foreword

A cartoon in a recent issue of the *Saturday Review* shows the Viking I Spaceship landed on Mars and reaching vainly in the general direction of a dark hole from which many pairs of eyes peer in consternation. Then one of the creatures whispers, "If we all keep quiet, maybe they'll think there's no one here."

Probably they are Torch Lighters with wet matches, narrowly escaping a survey resulting in twenty-two recommendations for better performance of their duties. And that is not all. In another dozen years, a Viking will be back to check on whether they did anything about their shortcomings or whether they remain in a hole and in the dark. Are their matches dry now? Have they found a more abrasive stone for the strike?

It took a lot of courage for anyone to investigate the preparation of teachers of reading in the first place, almost as much as it did to participate in the survey. Each teacher-educator had had such privacy before! His secret formula for success had been as well guarded as the solutions of problems which early mathematicians kept to themselves.

It took even more courage to return to the same population to find out their progress and their recommendations for further changes. (Twenty-six percent of that population did not respond to the second questionnaire. I know: you think "wet matches"; but it could be that they are so busy making changes, scoping their sequences, interweaving classroom teaching experiences with modules and oddsbodules, matching personalities with always one left over, that they had no time to answer.)

Torch Lighters Revisited is not an attempt to standardize and shape the teacher-educator. Rather, it is a book of helpful ideas for you to measure against the ones you already have, and perhaps add to your collection. It is a nudge and reminder that we have still a way to go for perfection in the development of teachers of reading. In the dark it is easy to keep going in circles. (One of the new recommendations in *Torch Lighters Revisited* was a common practice forty years ago, abandoned on the advent of General Education. I feel vindicated!)

Coleman Morrison and Mary Austin have done us all a great service of a quality that we have come to expect from them. For you, for future teachers, for the International Reading Association, and for myself, I thank my good friends and admired colleagues, Mary and Cole, for making this survey available to us on Earth. Mars has no idea what it's missing.

CONSTANCE M. MCCULLOUGH

Introduction

The Torch Lighters Revisited is a follow up of the original study published in 1961 when Johnny's teacher's teachers were the subject of intense scrutiny. Since colleges of education assume the major responsibility for preparing prospective teachers of reading, the study was undertaken to determine how well this objective was being met and, where weaknesses were noted, to make recommendations for improving that preparation.

Subsequently, twenty-two recommendations were made dealing with a multitude of areas that began with entrance requirements and ended with exit and follow up considerations. Of the recommendations, Francis Keppel, then Dean of the Harvard Graduate School of Education, wrote in his foreword to the original *The Torch Lighters:*

> They deserve the careful attention of school and college officials alike, and I hope they will be widely discussed and acted upon. The nation cannot afford to neglect them (i:xv).

In an effort to determine the extent to which the recommendations have been adopted or modified and to determine what additional changes have taken place in teacher preparatory programs in recent years, a modified follow up of *The Torch Lighters* was undertaken in Spring 1974, consisting of a three-part questionnaire concerned with three broad areas:

1. The extent of adoption of the original twenty-two recommendations made in *The Torch Lighters.*
2. Significant changes that had taken place in recent years in colleges and universities where prospective teachers of reading were being prepared.
3. Suggested recommendations for the future as indicated by respondents to the questionnaire.

The questionnaire was mailed to 220 schools, including the 74 colleges and universities that participated in the field study of *The Torch Lighters.* A total of 161 respondents (73.2 percent of the population) returned completed questionnaires. These schools were located in forty states and were considered to be representative of the various institutions where prospective teachers of reading are being prepared.

Apart from questionnaire information, fifty schools were selected to give more detailed information about their programs and, in some instances, to be interviewed by the study staff.

And what do the results reveal? Part 1 indicates that a majority of the recommendations were in effect, including many believed to be the most germane (e.g., that the equivalent of a three hour course in reading be required of prospective teachers of reading). In other instances, the recommendation not only had been adopted but had been superseded. Many schools were requiring a second and a third course in reading. In addition, much more emphasis was being placed on teaching selected aspects of diagnosis at the under-graduate level. In the previous study, such a course was usually considered to have only graduate level status. Yet, despite advances, little progress appears to have been made in some areas of preparation. This is notable in the case of student teaching programs considered by some to be essential for the preparatory approach. The present study indicates that little effort is being made to attract quality teachers in the role of "cooperating" teachers, and that colleges rarely recognize, either financially or professionally, the responsibilities assumed by those teachers who do induct the student teacher in her first teaching experience.

Part 2 of the study was concerned with changes that have taken place recently in teacher preparatory programs. Over four-fifths of the respondents revealed that such changes did, in fact, take place. The most predominant changes dealt with 1) the scope of the reading programs (more courses, more specialization opportunities, and broader content coverage); 2) content (where the emphasis was focused on competency based performances, the use of modules, and the movement of courses from the campus to the more realistic setting of the public schools); and 3) related experiences (the most noteworthy being observation and tutorial programs).

Part 3 of the study dealt with recommendations for the future as determined by the respondents. Slightly less than one-half of the respondents attempted to cope with this area. Where their recommendations extended beyond the original ones in *The Torch Lighters*, they were concerned with 1) an increase in the number of required courses from one to two (and in some instances, to three or four), 2) an earlier introduction of the student to realistic reading settings and interaction with children (as early as the freshman year in some recommendations), 3) the quality of faculty responsible for teaching reading courses, and 4) the need for federal funding to subsidize both the prospective teacher and teacher preparatory programs.

Chapter 4 introduces two descriptions of teacher education programs in reading at the undergraduate level. The first illustrates a carefully planned, competency based alternative for the single required reading course offered in College A. Several elements of competency based instruction have been included: 1) prestatement of learner objectives and expected outcomes; 2) reliance upon instructional modules as course content; 3) personalized instruction with self-pacing and varied options among objectives, learning strategies, and postassessment procedures; 4) field-site schools where supervised classroom experiences take place; and 5) use of formative and summative evaluations in program revisions.

The second illustration is a model in the true sense of the term, since it does not represent a program in any one location. As a composite of recommendations from several colleges and universities, College B reflects a number of promising practices based upon fact, theory, and professional expertise. As it is presented, the model offers a possible framework within which desired revisions can be accomplished.

We hope the entire report of *The Torch Lighters Revisited* will stimulate healthy debate and action for change in a time when alternatives for educating prospective teachers of reading are needed more than ever before.

Chapter 1

Status of the Recommendations

This part of the study deals with the extent to which recommendations have been put into effect, some representative comments provided by the respondents, and a brief discussion of both the results and the accompanying comments. In presenting this information, some reporting problems did emerge and these are discussed in Appendix B.

Recommendation 1

That all students be required to make formal application to teacher education programs at the end of the sophomore year—selection criteria to include degree of academic proficiency, mental and emotional maturity, indication of aptitude for teaching, and competency in the elementary grade skills.

RESULTS

	N	%
1. in effect	92	57.1
2. modified or strengthened	45	28.0
3. not in effect	19	11.8
4. not applicable	4	2.5
5. no response	1	0.6
	161	100.0

REPRESENTATIVE COMMENTS

"Formal application for professional education initiated during freshman and sophomore years and not later than second semester of sophomore year."

"We admit in freshman year, using high school rank and ACT scores."

"All of the above plus a required field experience."

"We have all criteria named except emotional maturity. This is subjectively judged through letters of recommendation and interview."

"No formal testing is conducted; students are interviewed."

"New plans for selecting prospective students will be implemented and include competencies listed above as well as a successful completion of a preprofessional seminar during freshman or sophomore year."

"The cost to do this in a rigid manner, using the best screening procedures available would be prohibitive, and politically impossible."

"Students must also have completed a successful field experience in order to be admitted to our teacher education program."

"We had such application apparatus but dropped it because it became unmanageable."

DISCUSSION

The intent of this recommendation was to upgrade the criteria used to determine which students should be admitted to programs where prospective elementary school teachers are educated. The results appear to indicate that the recommendation has been put into effect to a substantial extent. Indeed, a few respondents indicated, in addition, speech and hearing tests, seminars, and field experiences. These field experiences are discussed more fully in Chapter Three.

Modifications of the recommendation generally represent a change of time as to when the selection criteria should be applied. Whereas the recommendation suggested the end of the sophomore year, many respondents indicated that this process took place considerably earlier; in some schools as early as the freshman year. Other colleges and universities, although fewer in number, indicated a delay in the screening process due to the large number of transfer students who did not enroll in their educational programs until after the sophomore year.

Other modifications of the recommendation include the omission of assessment techniques for mental and emotional maturity and/or aptitude for teaching. Clearly, the predominant theme surrounding this omission is the lack of faith in the validity and reliability of available assessment instruments. Others cite the cost of objective testing as a deterrent to adoption. These two factors presumably explain the general utilization of subjective measures when efforts are made to screen candidates for maturation and attitude attributes. Such decisions are usually made on the basis of a personal interview, a screening device that is apparently being used to a greater extent now than at the time of the original field study. While this technique is considered extremely useful, it is admittedly more feasible in colleges which are not overwhelmed by large numbers of applicants.

Recommendation 2

That students be permitted (if not encouraged) to elect a field of concentration other than elementary education, provided basic requirements in the education program are met, including the equivalent of a three semester hour course in the teaching of reading and one course in student teaching.

RESULTS

	N	%
1. in effect	88	54.7
2. modified or strengthened	43	26.7
3. not in effect	21	13.0
4. not applicable	8	5.0
5. no response	1	0.6
	161	100.0

REPRESENTATIVE COMMENTS

"Field of concentration other than elementary education is *required* of all majors."

"We require at least a minor in another field and generally a major. We require 6 hours in reading."

"Students are required to elect a 24 points concentration in a liberal studies area. In addition, students take 6 points in the teaching of reading and 2 student teaching experiences."

"All elementary education majors are required to take two three-semester hour courses in Reading Methods (the courses are prescribed). They may also elect a concentration of 18 s.h. in Reading or enter the Reading Collateral program of 24 s. h."

"All our students earn a major in a subject area."

"40 core elementary education, 40 hours electives with at least one concentration—a new program this year."

"A field of concentration other than elementary education is required."

"No one pursuing an elementary curriculum can major or minor in elementary education."

"Students are required to elect a field of concentration other than elementary education; in addition to the equivalent of a three-semester hour course in reading required, a concentration in reading may be taken as an elective (18 hrs.)"

"Under California credential legislation, a student must major in a field other than elementary education. A student has no choice in the matter."

This recommendation had a twofold purpose: 1) to allow those students who had an interest in a particular field of study outside of elementary education (e.g., anthropology) to be permitted to major in that subject, and 2) to focus attention on the need for college graduates to attain a degree of sophistication in both academic and professional courses of study. Admittedly, this is often difficult to accomplish within the confines of a four year degree program. On the other hand, many colleges do allow students the option of enrolling in a multitude of elective courses (as many as 40 hours in some schools) so there appears to be no valid reason for a student to jeopardize one strand of education at the expense of another.

Results indicate that the recommendation is in effect in a large percentage of the schools sampled, and supporting comments are noteworthy on two points: 1) numerous schools now *require* a field of concentration other than elementary education, and 2) students are required to enroll in *more* than a three semester hour course in the teaching of reading. In several instances additional reading courses can lead to a "major" or a "specialization" in that area. Under such circumstances, it is difficult to see how students can complete a major in reading instruction as well as additional requirements in elementary education and still have sufficient electives to be eligible for a second major outside their professional studies sequence. Although this would appear to be in contradistinction to the intent of the recommendation, it should be pointed out that the original study (1:142) said: "While a majority of prospective elementary school teachers will probably elect education as their field of concentration, there are some who...will want to major in a liberal arts subject...[and] there would seem to be no valid reason to discourage such a noneducation major."

Apart from the availability of specialized reading programs, there also appears to be a trend toward the requirements of two reading courses at the baccalaureate level.

Recommendation 3

That those faculty members charged with the responsibility for training prospective teachers make every effort to inculcate in their students a sense of pride in their chosen profession.

	N	%
1. in effect	131	81.4
2. modified or strengthened	23	14.3
3. not in effect	6	3.7
4. not applicable	1	0.6
5. no response	0	0.0
	161	100.0

REPRESENTATIVE COMMENTS

"This is being done by some faculty members. I question the attitudes of others and, therefore, their ability to do this."

"I am well impressed by our faculty in this respect. There is a real effort shown by the faculty who are themselves proud of their profession."

"We also encourage membership in professional organizations including IRA. There is a CSU local chapter."

"Current teacher shortage has brought the realization that prospective teachers had better begin to recognize the need to be enthusiastic and energetic for teaching. Their professors share this feeling."

"Sorrowfully, I do not see this attitude prevalent at this time."

DISCUSSION

The rationale for this recommendation resulted from the contention that teaching, as a profession, was not considered to be highly regarded either by lay persons or by teachers themselves and that more effective efforts would have to be made to enhance the status and dignity of the position.

Results of the present study indicate overwhelming endorsement for the recommendation. In instances where responses indicated that a stronger version of the recommendation was in effect, the evidence included the involvement of students in professional organizations (such as the International Reading Association), attendance at state sponsored reading conferences and local reading councils, and involvement in collegiate teacher related organizations such as Future Teachers of America and Phi Delta Kappa.

Recommendation 4

That senior faculty members, prominent in the field of reading, play a more active role in the instruction of undergraduates and assume responsibility for teaching at least one undergraduate course.

	N	%
1. in effect	117	72.7
2. modified or strengthened	28	17.4
3. not in effect	10	6.2
4. not applicable	4	2.5
5. no response	2	1.2
	161	100.0

REPRESENTATIVE COMMENTS

"We have three faculty members with doctorates in reading. They teach all of the undergraduate reading courses."

"Situation described above predates *The Torch Lighters.*"

"As much as possible within staffing limitations."

"This varies from year to year according to what faculty is available."

"*Only* senior faculty members teach undergraduate reading course."

"We have no graduate faculty designated as such. Our senior faculty all participate heavily in undergraduate instruction."

"We either teach undergraduates or work closely with the lecturers who do. Our lecturers are all doctoral students in reading and get valuable experience by teaching under supervision. Most will be teaching reading at the college level."

DISCUSSION

It was observed frequently during the initial study that faculty members considered to be authorities in the field of reading were likely to be engaged in graduate teaching and research projects to the exclusion of any involvement in the baccalaureate programs. The study staff lamented the fact that many prospective teachers, therefore, did not benefit from the expertise and knowledge of leaders in the area of reading and recommended that undergraduate students have the option of enrolling in at least one course taught by a highly trained and experienced professor.

With only ten exceptions, this recommendation is in effect and respondents expressed positive reactions to the proposal. Obviously, as indicated in some of the comments, staffing problems occasionally arise which preclude senior faculty from teaching an undergraduate course every semester. Similarly, senior faculty on study leaves or sabbaticals are not always available. Nevertheless, the recommendation has over 90 percent endorsement.

Recommendation 5

That the class time devoted to reading instruction, whether taught as a separate course or integrated with the language arts, be equivalent to at least three semester hours of credit.

RESULTS

	N	%
1. in effect	108	67.1
2. modified or strengthened	44	27.3
3. not in effect	5	3.1
4. not applicable	4	2.5
5. no response	0	0.0
	161	100.0

REPRESENTATIVE COMMENTS

"Current requirements are six hours in reading, i.e., teaching of diagnosis, plus three hours in language arts."

"Most of our students take at least one additional course in reading other than the basic one."

"Six semester hours of credit in reading is required of all elementary majors."

"We presently require six hours: three in general methods and another three in a practicum related to student teaching."

"Require six semester hours: developmental and remedial reading."

"This is a required minimum; rarely does a student take less than fifteen semester hours, although we are on a quarter system."

"Two three-semester-hour courses in Teaching of Reading are required for all elementary education students."

DISCUSSION

During the first study it was reported that 97 percent of the colleges sampled required a course in basic reading instruction. In approximately half of these, it was taught as a separate course and usually carried three semester hours of credit. In the remaining half, it was taught as an integrated course (with other components of the language arts) when 10-25 percent of the class time, or approximately four and one-half to eleven and one-quarter class hours, was spent specifically on reading instruction. With such minimal exposure to reading instruction, in the case of the integrated course, the staff recommended that students be exposed to at least the equivalent of forty-five class hours.

An examination of the results indicates that not only has the recommendation been put into effect by a large percentage of schools sampled but numerous respondents indicate that an equivalent three semester credit course now is only the minimum requirement. It is not uncommon that six or more semester hours credit are required and that the elective course offerings in reading are considerably more extensive than before. With the introduction of additional courses in reading, it is possible for students in some colleges to specialize or major in reading (see discussion of recommendation 2).

In those schools where reading is not given as much emphasis as recommended in the guidelines, respondents indicated they were hoping to offer the equivalent of a three semester credit course in the future.

Recommendation 6

That the basic reading instruction offered to prospective elementary teachers be broadened to include content and instructional techniques appropriate for the intermediate and upper grades.

RESULTS

	N	%
1. in effect	127	78.9
2. modified or strengthened	28	17.4
3. not in effect	4	2.5
4. not applicable	2	1.2
5. no response	0	0.0
	161	100.0

REPRESENTATIVE COMMENTS

"Reading instruction appropriate for the middle grades required for all except early childhood education majors."

"Our course is designed for grades one through eight and includes these instructional techniques."

"The second three-semester-hour course, which is required of all elementary education majors, includes content and instructional techniques appropriate for intermediate grades."

"Our second course is content reading and oriented to upper elementary and junior high students."

"This is impossible in a three semester hour course, which is what we have at the present time."

"Our program is much stronger. We require four courses in elementary education—one devoted to the reading skills appropriate for grades four through eight."

The previous study listed three reasons for the inclusion of this ecommendation: 1) an overemphasis on beginning reading which precluded course time for advanced skills; 2) apathy on the part of he instructor to offer substantial instruction in intermediate grade eading skills, and 3) lack of background on the part of the students to absorb instruction. Of these, the first was presumably the most predominant reason for the limited amount of time devoted to intermediate grade reading instruction. A glance at the topics receiving he most emphasis in the college reading courses, at the time of the original study, reveals that four of the first five topics are related to beginning reading instruction.

Initially, one might find acceptance of this recommendation somewhat surprising. However, considering the expanded course offerings in reading and the widespread adoption of a three semester credit course in reading as a minimum, it is evident that increased time for reading instruction has brought about some balance of emphasis between primary and intermediate instruction. Another hopeful sign is the absence of any comments restricting reading instruction to initial reading in order to accommodate slower students.

Recommendation 7

That college instructors continue to emphasize that no one method of word recognition, such as phonic analysis, be used to the exclusion of other word attack techniques.

That students be exposed to a variety of opinions related to other significant issues of reading, such as grouping policies, prereading materials, techniques of beginning reading instruction, and teaching machines.

RESULTS	N	%
1. in effect	137	85.1
2. modified or strengthened	19	11.8
3. not in effect	2	1.2
4. not applicable	3	1.9
5. no response	0	0.0
	161	100.0

"We have a series of reading courses, including one called Issues an[...] Trends in Elementary School Reading."

"We even offer seminars (voluntary) on controversial topics."

"We do this. In our state, however, there is pressure to emphasiz[...] the right method—phonics!"

"Yes, and students often object that they are not getting *the* answe[...] and *the* way. Many would be more satisfied if we promoted on[...] method only."

"More varieties of reading course offerings provide more latitude i[...] these areas."

"Most have recognized the futility of narrowing the thinking of thei[...] students."

"We have a staff of ten, eight with doctorates, who were chosen be[...] cause they believe in different approaches to the teaching of read[...] ing. Students cannot progress through the program without meeting at least three points of view, and they occasionally complain be[...] cause they are taught conflicting beliefs."

"We would take a different approach, emphasizing the method o[...] reading that fits best with our overall philosophy of teaching and learning."

DISCUSSION

Considering the publication date of the original study, one ca[...] easily recall the public and professional furor which prevailed ove[...] the issue of phonic analysis and, in particular, whether it was bein[...] employed as a word attack skill. During the past fifteen years, [...] plethora of research has supported the point of view that childre[...] learn to decode unknown words by a variety of methods—mos[...] notably through a combination of phonic, structural, and con[...] textual analysis. Consequently, few would argue with the con[...] tention that there is no one method by which children learn t[...] master the act of decoding. Similarly, with other controversial issue[...] of the early sixties—homogeneous versus heterogeneous grouping early versus delayed introduction to initial reading instruction, the adoption of one methodological approach over another—there i[...] almost universal consensus that no particular approach, set of ma[...] terials, or doctrine could apply equally well to all readers.

Thus it is not surprising that there is overwhelming adoption o[...] this recommendation, even to the extent that several colleges offe[...] separate courses to acquaint their students with the controversia[...] issues of the times. It is also interesting to note that representative comments occasionally indicate that some undergraduate students still ask to be informed of the *one* method of teaching reading.

Recommendation 8

That college instructors take greater responsibility in making certain that their students have mastered the principles of phonic and structural analysis.

RESULTS

	N	%
1. in effect	110	68.3
2. modified or strengthened	35	21.7
3. not in effect	12	7.5
4. not applicable	4	2.5
5. no response	0	0.0
	161	100.0

REPRESENTATIVE COMMENTS

"Difficult to respond to this one because of the word *greater*. Greater than what?"

"A mid term exam in the required reading course measures this through syllabicating words and placing primary accents."

"Methods students are required to complete a programed text on word attack skills."

"All students are expected to pass a proficiency (instructor made) check."

"All students are required to demonstrate their competency in phonic analysis, structural analysis, and context analysis."

"Our new competency based teacher education focus in reading will help to meet this need."

"Students in the first course in reading are required to pass a knowledge proficiency test in phonics and structural analysis."

"We have modularized two undergraduate courses to include mastery units in word analysis and others. Course credit is withheld until they establish proficiency."

"This gets varying degrees of emphasis; some of us just don't believe in the accepted versions of principles and are much more concerned with other aspects of learning to read."

DISCUSSION

This recommendation was based on the initial finding that many teachers were not helping their pupils to use a variety of word analysis skills because, as teachers, they were often deficient in some of these skills themselves. In particular they lacked knowledge of many components of phonic and structural analysis (presumably, because they had never been taught these skills). Therefore, when a child encountered an unknown word most teachers tended to tell him what the word was, or ask other peers to decode the word. Under these circumstances, it did not appear that children were developing into self-reliant, discriminating readers. Also there was no concentrated effort in the early sixties to ensure that prospective teachers were familiar with a variety of word analysis techniques.

Based on the results, it would appear that today's college professors are assuming more responsibility for ensuring that the teaching of word attack skills is included in the curriculum. Judging from the representative comments of the respondents, many colleges of education have established numerous assessment devices to measure a student's proficiency in this area of reading knowledge.

Recommendation 9

That a course in basic reading instruction be required of all *prospective secondary school teachers.*

RESULTS

	N	%
1. in effect	40	24.8
2. modified or strengthened	24	14.9
3. not in effect	78	48.4
4. not applicable	15	9.3
5. no response	4	2.5
	161	99.9

REPRESENTATIVE COMMENTS

"New Ryan Bill for credential teachers. California requires this."

"This is now state law in Kentucky."

"Effective in Wisconsin, 1977."

"All English teachers now required to take this course."

"Not required of all on our campus, only for social studies and English majors."

"All secondary majors in communication skills are required to take a course in secondary school reading; it is an elective for the other majors."

"Required of those with English majors or minors only."

"Not required but is available; many advisors of secondary education majors in various fields require the course."

"In fact, the state of Pennsylvania has dropped this as a requirement and a secondary reading vacancy has not been filled."

"Secondary reading course is offered in the elective form."

"Not required at this time."

"This course was dropped in the early sixties."

"No longer required by all."

"Recommended but not yet in effect."

"Unfortunately we haven't penetrated the crustiness of the secondary education department."

"We have tried and, so far, have failed."

"A course in basic reading instruction is required of prospective English teachers only."

"Have discussed the need. No action to date."

DISCUSSION

If one would combine responses in columns one and two from the questionnaire, the indication would be that this recommendation was in effect at approximately 40 percent of the schools sampled. However, this is one example where the respondents who have checked column two are indicating a modification of the recommendation rather than a strengthening of it. In almost every instance, as supported by the accompanying comments, the modification relates to the elimination of the emphasized word *all* in the recommendation. What the respondents are saying is that prospective teachers of secondary school English and, in some instances, prospective secondary social studies teachers are required to enroll in a basic reading course but that this requirement does not apply to *all* prospective secondary school teachers. Therefore, although the results shown above indicate that the recommendation is not in effect in 48 percent of the colleges sampled, the figure rises to 63 percent when the responses in columns two and three are combined. When one further eliminates the 9 percent of respondents who indicated that the recommendation was not applicable to their schools (primarily because of the absence of a secondary school program), the percentage of schools not requiring prospective secondary school teachers to enroll in a basic reading course increases to an even higher percentage.

But there is a hopeful sign that this high percentage will diminish somewhat in subsequent years. In Wisconsin, for example, a state law will go into effect in 1977 mandating that graduates majoring in secondary education will not qualify for a teaching certificate without a reading course. Other states have prepared similar legislation, but one questions why such requirements did not originate with colleges and universities rather than with state legislatures.

Until such laws are enacted or put into effect, or until college of education make the changes, many secondary school pupils wi be denied opportunities for increasing their reading skills. Man teachers do not have adequate training for helping their studen improve reading skills or for diagnosing and correcting readin problems. Thus, for many children, it appears that the elementar school will continue to be a terminal point in the development c reading progress.

Recommendation 10

That colleges offer a course, or inservice training, in reading in struction specifically designed for principals, supervisors, and co operating teachers.

RESULTS

	N	%
1. in effect	50	31.
2. modified or strengthened	22	13.
3. not in effect	68	42.
4. not applicable	18	11.
5. no response	3	1.
	161	100.

REPRESENTATIVE COMMENTS

"As part of master's degree."

"Offered as a graduate course."

"We haven't offered such a course. Might be a good idea. Pre sumably, if they earned their job titles, reading was stressed in their background courses and experiences."

"Not a specific course for just that group. Twenty-one hours o graduate work available in reading."

"Not a course, but a practicum in the administration/supervision o public school reading programs."

"This will be started next year on a voluntary basis."

"A graduate course, Organization and Administration of the Reading Program, is open to school administrators and/or school reading specialists."

"Four reading courses being taught in school districts as part of inservice, plus statewide Right to Read training program with seventy participants."

"We don't have a specific course but we do offer various extension courses and on campus courses in reading open to principals, supervisors, and cooperating teachers in reading."

"We would like to do this but our staff is too limited. There are too few principals and supervisors who want to improve their reading skills."

"Chief school administrators no longer have to take a course in reading."

SCUSSION

Considering the fact that during the original field study the aff noted the absence of any viable inservice educational programs ecause too often administrators in a responsible position were not fficiently informed about the complexities of reading instruction component skills), the recommendation has considerable merit. retrospect, however, it does not have a practical application to e baccalaureate program and undoubtedly accounts for the fact at a majority of respondents indicated it was either not in effect or t applicable.

On the other hand, the accompanying comments indicate that any courses are offered at the *graduate* level and, although not designed specifically for them, school administrators are encouraged enroll in the courses.

In the final analysis, the trend in offering off-campus courses in public school setting may prove more conducive to the enrollment administrative staff in graduate reading courses.

Recommendation 11

. *That more use be made of the case study or problem centered approach so that students are given the opportunity to relate theory to a particular problem and ultimately to analyze, interpret, and solve that problem.*

. *That tape recordings and films of classroom activities be utilized to supplement course offerings.*

. *That students be provided with directed observational experiences in local schools concurrently with their course work in reading, or that they have the opportunity of observing classroom teaching on closed circuit television.*

. *That college administrators make every effort to coordinate reading instruction with the practice teaching program.*

RESULTS*

| | Part A | | Part B | | Part C | | Part D | |
	N	%	N	%	N	%	N	%
1. in effect	98	60.9	98	60.9	106	65.8	93	5'
2. modified or strengthened	44	27.3	41	25.5	40	24.8	35	2.
3. not in effect	14	8.7	14	8.7	10	6.2	24	1
4. not applicable	5	3.1	7	4.3	4	2.5	7	
5. no response	0	0.0	1	0.6	1	0.6	2	
	161	100.0	161	100.0	161	99.9	161	99

REPRESENTATIVE COMMENTS

"Instead of limiting students to observation, they either particip in a field experience or a resident tutor program."

"Students take methods courses on Monday and Wednesday and a in schools Tuesday and Thursday supervised by a methods prof sor."

"Almost all preservice instruction has been moved off campus for onsite teacher education program; student-pupil tutorials are r quired in all sections of reading courses."

"Related laboratory experiences are incorporated as a component the course work in the junior year."

"Problem solving techniques are more likely to be undertak during advanced classes which are not taken by all students. St dents in reading clinic courses are videotaped while teaching ar then given an opportunity to evaluate themselves. Item D to a sm extent only."

"Much of this can be accomplished through our field centered pr gram where the public schools become our laboratory."

"We do much of our own filming and offer our students an o portunity to react to it. We are not yet able to afford commercial prepared films, nor do we think they are as functional as 'hom made' ones."

"Too few staff members is the limiting factor here."

"We have tape recorded and filmed examples of 'good' and 'poo teaching techniques, and our students assess the strengths and wea nesses of both."

*See also Appendix C.

During the original field study, members of the team visiting ollege campuses frequently requested an opportunity to observe a lass in reading instruction. As a result of these observations, they oted that there was heavy reliance on the use of the lecture method nd little use made of audiovisual aids to supplement the lecture. he course was placed in the curriculum at a time when students ad had no previous opportunity to observe in cooperating classooms (1:148). The net result was frustration to instructor and stuents alike: to the instructor, because he feared that his students did ot have a firm understanding of the concepts being presented, and the students because they comprehended little of an unfamiliar eory that appeared to have no practical value.

As the present results clearly indicate, numerous changes have ken place in the intervening years. Perhaps the most effective ove toward overcoming the problems of lecture hall instruction as to leave the campus setting for a public school setting and rovide reading instruction in conjunction with observations and utorial programs. Even those lecturers who did not opt for this exediency have come to the realization that reading instruction canot be taught in a vacuum divorced from practical application, as umerous respondents indicated.

Of the four internal suggestions made, the most widely adopted y more than 90 percent of the colleges sampled) was the use of bservation techniques either before or with reading instruction. roblem solving techniques are similarly in effect, although they are ore likely to be found in graduate programs. Tape recordings and lms of local origin are widely used, especially for diagnosis. Reondents indicated that the high cost of commercial films preuded their purchase or rental.

While a strong majority indicate that efforts are made to cordinate reading instruction with practice teaching programs, reonses to other parts of this study seem to indicate that these efforts ave not necessarily been translated into reality.

Looking at the overall results, one can conclude that more nstructors are moving away from the "traditional" method of intructor/pupil communication that was found to be so prevalent uring observations in the original study. It would now be of nterest to know what effect on the student this transition has had, oth in terms of acquisition of knowledge and subsequent perormance in the classroom.

Recommendation 12

That all prospective teachers become acquainted with technique,
interpretation, and evaluation of current and past research.

That all prospective teachers be introduced to professional reading
journals.

RESULTS*

	Part A		Part B	
	N	%	N	%
1. in effect	86	53.4	99	61.
2. modified or strengthened	39	24.2	38	23.
3. not in effect	33	20.4	22	13.
4. not applicable	3	1.9	2	1.
5. no response	0	0.0	0	0.
	161	99.9	161	100.

REPRESENTATIVE COMMENTS

"Varies from course to course as to research emphasis."

"Undergraduate students required to take course in Fundamental
of Research."

"Done only on a graduate level."

"Undergraduates get latter, but little of former."

"These skills given low priority in a three credit course."

"Both of these are done through assignments, although it is difficul
to emphasize techniques of research. More attention is given to in
terpretation and application of results."

"Prospective elementary school teachers get very little research, bu
prospective secondary teachers do. The same is true of the second
half of this recommendation."

"We do this on a limited basis using the Eric/Crier/RRN material."

"Let's not try to make the undergraduate 'how to' course into a
graduate research course. Other than a few professional journals,
hesitate to cover research."

"Our psychology department offers this first portion of the recom
mendation as a separate course."

DISCUSSION

Since this recommendation consisted of two parts, a small
minority (10 percent of the respondents) chose to answer each sug
gestion separately. This point is made because, in the responses o

*See also Appendix C.

ese sixteen, a sharp distinction was made between acquainting
ıdents with selected aspects of research (which clearly was not
)ne) and introducing students to professional reading journals
·hich obviously was done). One is therefore led to speculate
hether a similar dichotomy might have emerged had all reondents reacted to separate parts of the recommendation as op-
)sed to treating it in its entirety.

There is a controversy among the respondents over the pre-
ntation of research at the undergraduate level, although it is not
ıite clear how this can be entirely avoided if students are expected
read and interpret the professional journals.

In reviewing the rationale for the recommendation, it is
ident that it was not intended that students probe deeply into the
·eas of research but that students be given "enough training in
chniques to enable them to participate in cooperative research
ıntures within their schools, to view research findings with some
:gree of professional skill, to determine the importance of the re-
ılts for their own use, and to evaluate the findings in light of their
ttended purpose" (1:149). In retrospect, that seems to be a rather
vesome task for undergraduates! Without access to *The Torch
ighters* or a knowledge of its contents, respondents probably would
ot have attributed such a global definition to the recommendation.
n the other hand, if they had access—and the recommendation is
ıe reality in colleges as indicated—then it would appear that the
ıillennium may not be too far away.

ecommendation 13

*'hat the staff responsible for teaching reading and/or language arts
ourses be sufficiently augmented to allow each instructor time in
>hich to observe and confer with students during the practice
:aching experience and to consult with the cooperating teacher and
dministrative personnel.*

ESULTS

	N	%
1. in effect	53	32.9
2. modified or strengthened	24	14.9
3. not in effect	71	44.1
4. not applicable	12	7.5
5. no response	1	0.6
	161	100.0

"The student teaching and method courses are two entirely differe[nt] things. You are not teaching the same student that you are worki[ng] with in student teaching."

"This is a strong university policy."

"At present, unless we are engaged in student teaching supervisio[n] this is not done. Two schools have field based programs. In the[se] schools, this is done."

"Our required reading practicum for both elementary and secon[d]ary students (each, three hour courses) include what you ha[ve] described above."

"All are invited to participate but are not assigned."

"The above is true for prospective elementary teachers but not f[or] prospective high school teachers."

"Reading staff is in reasonably close touch with students during st[u]dent teaching."

"We have a division of labor, but the director of student teachin[g] teaches the reading course and chooses the supervisors."

"Student teaching and reading are separated with little interaction[.]"

"The student teachers are generally supervised by faculty membe[rs] who do not teach any of the reading courses."

"During reading participation experience, but not necessaril[y] during student teaching."

"The staff in reading and language arts is actively involved with th[e] supervision of student teachers but, with the numbers in our readin[g] classes, it is impossible to follow all students into student teaching."

"Course teaching load circumvents the time necessary for readin[g] instructors to be able to follow through."

"Great idea. We face budget reality here, however. Sorry to have t[o] report 'Torch Dimming' at this time."

"This happens occasionally, but we are under such budget stress an[d] teaching overloads that it does not happen regularly. We do, how[-]ever, require miniteaching in several quarters prior to studen[t] teaching and the interchange does take place there."

"Visitations are made but, with 500 students scattered around th[e] state each semester, this is not too practical."

"Instructors do this as a part of their four required hours of advisor[y] time per week."

DISCUSSION

This recommendation stemmed from a relatively standard pro[-]cedure in which students enrolled in a basic reading course taugh[t] by one instructor and were supervised in their student teaching ex[-]perience by another. Often, these college instructors were member[s]

f different departments and did not have the opportunity and/or
ıe desire to communicate with one another. Thus, a student might
ttempt to practice what had been learned in a reading course and
ıen be criticized for those very practices by the student teaching
ıpervisor. The original study indicated "that about half of the
ading instructors queried during the field study did not supervise
ıeir students during the practice teaching experience." The study
vent on to point out, "Indeed, many of them [reading instructors]
ıldom visited the cooperating local classrooms to observe the
ıethodology practiced there" (1:150).

Although the populations of the original and follow up studies
re somewhat different, the results today appear to be similar to
vhat they were yesterday. Indeed the comments of respondents
ıdicate that the recommendation as stated may not be in effect to
he extent implied. Most of the modifications to the recommenda-
ion relate to sporadic observations by reading instructors in local
chools during tutorial programs related more closely to reading and
rereading courses than to student teaching. This modification is a
omewhat different concept than that envisioned by the study staff
vhen the recommendation was originally made. Budgetary con-
iderations, staffing problems, and time continue to be cited as bar-
iers precluding significant progress toward the realization of the
ecommendation.

Recommendation 14

*That additional experimental research be initiated in the areas of
critical reading, study skills, and grouping practices.*

RESULTS

	N	%
1. in effect	35	21.7
2. modified or strengthened	20	12.4
3. not in effect	80	50.0
4. not applicable	15	9.3
5. no response	11	6.8
	161	100.2

REPRESENTATIVE COMMENTS

"This is a nebulous item. All would agree with it, but who should do
this, the college instructor?"

"By whom? For whom?"

"Most faculty members contribute to journals or professional con ventions."

"At least two faculty members have been engaged in the seriou study of the process of critical reading and have developed a cours on the teaching of critical reading."

"Only these areas? We are working in many others; these are spe areas!"

"No research, but these topics are each discussed."

"Experimental research for the advanced graduate student. Man other topics could be added."

"We have not found it possible to do experimental research of th nature at the undergraduate level."

"Not one of our thrusts. May develop if staff increases."

"Faculty assignments at this institution have allowed for little re search. Some small attention is given through dissertation research but this has been mostly in beginning reading."

"Research is an individual choice in this university and is done b individual professors in these areas."

DISCUSSION

This recommendation was an outgrowth of field study inter views with reading professors who indicated that their instruction: presentation would be strengthened if more empirical data wer available relative to specific aspects of reading such as those in dicated in the recommendation. As with Recommendation 10, on can perhaps understand why this recommendation may have bee made but it is more difficult to relate it specifically to the bac calaureate preparatory program. It is not surprising that this recom mendation is not in effect in a majority of the schools sampled an the comments of the respondents do not need additional discussion

Recommendation 15

a. *That the colleges recruit, train, and certify cooperating teachers*

b. *That cooperating teachers, after training and college certifica tion, serve in the capacity of associates to the college.*

c. *That as associates to the college, cooperating teachers participat in the formulation of practice teaching programs, in relatec seminars, and in the final evaluation of student performance.*

d. *That as associates to the college, cooperating teachers receiv financial remuneration commensurate with their roles.*

Chapter On

	Part A		Part B		Part C		Part D	
	N	%	N	%	N	%	N	%
1. in effect	35	21.7	25	15.5	36	22.3	42	26.1
2. modified or strengthened	24	14.9	18	11.1	25	15.5	24	14.9
3. not in effect	77	47.8	93	57.8	77	47.8	73	45.3
4. not applicable	20	12.4	23	14.2	20	12.4	19	11.8
5. no response	5	3.1	2	1.2	3	1.9	3	1.8
	161	99.9	161	99.8	161	99.9	161	99.9

REPRESENTATIVE COMMENTS

"The school systems receive credits which teachers can use for tuition toward graduate work."

"C is done to some degree on a voluntary basis."

"Several public school personnel are borrowed each year for supervisory roles."

"Cooperating teachers participate in final evaluation of student performance and receive financial remuneration (not commensurate with their work). The extent of their participation in planning is limited."

"All cooperating teachers receive $200 from the state of Texas for working with one or more student teachers during the academic year."

"Cooperating teachers are required to take training and are actively involved in developing the program objectives. They validate performance objectives and recommend additional training for individuals."

"The rules and regulations of the university do not permit cooperating teachers to serve in the capacity of associates to the university. However, the cooperating teachers and university supervisors cooperatively determine the student teaching program and student teaching grades."

"Very little of the above at the present time."

"Receive an honorarium paid by the student as a laboratory fee."

"Cooperating teachers receive a token payment; many believe they deserve more."

"We have moved, instead, to a teaching center scheme."

"We have an advisory board of twenty-four individuals from public schools. We use twelve local public teachers as supplementary teachers. We do inservice with public school teachers who work with student teachers."

*See also Appendix C.

"Have you tried to work with public schools?"

"We do have many public school teachers employed as adjun staff, and about one-half of our students spend two-thirds to o year in a public school where they work regularly with pupil teachers, and clinical professors."

"Unfortunately, when visiting cooperating schools we still s notices on the bulletin boards to the effect—who wants a stude teacher?"

DISCUSSION

In 1961, the staff of *The Torch Lighters* took the position tha "The practice teaching experience is considered the heart of tl teacher education program" (*1*:74). Presumably, the heartbeat w found in the person of the cooperating teacher who assumes maj responsibility for inducting the student teacher into practice teacl ing and guiding the apprentice through that program. Because the estimated influence exerted by the cooperating teacher on tl immediate as well as subsequent performance of the student, tl staff agreed that "it is essential that cooperating teachers be highl competent and well trained people.... This would necessitate tl development of a corps of specialists who not only are competer elementary school teachers but are specifically trained in the area instruction and supervision." (*1*:151-152). Where better to imple ment this proposal than within the colleges under whose jurisdictio the recruitment and education of cooperating teachers would tak place?

Results indicate that Part *D* of the recommendation has r ceived the highest percentage of acceptance among the college sampled although one could question whether a financial reward $50, $100, or $200 or tuition vouchers are, in fact, adequate r muneration in terms of the services they provide. Although man cooperating teachers are motivated purely through professional r sponsibilities, others would consider more tangible rewards as an in centive to participate in student teaching programs. Despite th widespread use of tuition vouchers, many teachers must forfeit thes because they have reached a terminal point in their education or ar unable to use them during the period specified (usually, tuitio vouchers are restricted to use during one academic year).

Although cooperating teachers still do not receive college statu to the extent intended in the recommendation, they do appear t have a more active role in the development of college policy con cerning student teaching programs. In spite of this trend, an over whelming majority still have no part in policy making decisions.

What is equally difficult to understand is that most colleges still o not recruit, train, or certify cooperating teachers. On the basis of lese findings, it would appear that the student teaching program, ften considered essential in teacher preparation, still has a long ay to go.

ecommendation 16

hat colleges appoint a liaison person to work directly with the local ;hool system to achieve closer cooperation between the schools and he college and to assist the public schools in upgrading reading and ther academic instruction.

ESULTS

	N	%
1. in effect	72	44.7
2. modified or strengthened	29	18.0
3. not in effect	48	29.8
4. not applicable	10	6.2
5. no response	2	1.2
	161	99.9

REPRESENTATIVE COMMENTS

"This is done, but not on a systematic basis."

"Public schools should appoint a liaison person."

"Our liaison persons are coordinators for the student teacher term— not exclusively reading, but involved with reading."

"Director of student teaching serves in this capacity."

"On request, the faculty in reading teach extension courses and in-service courses in reading for local school districts. They also serve on request as consultants in reading to local school districts."

"We have a coordinating committee to work with the schools."

"We have developed some teaching centers where we have a co-ordinator paid by the local schools."

"An assistant dean performs such functions with all cooperating school systems."

"Our student teaching supervisor is generally regarded as our liaison person."

"In one of the seven school systems where we send students, we have a liaison person who is employed half-time by the county and half-time by the university."

"Not enough staff."

"Insufficient budget. A faculty member responsible for this was not replaced."

As the original study pointed out on numerous occasions, close cooperation between the college and local schools was a worthy goal. Where rapport and mutual respect did not exist (as was often the case), the term "cooperating school" or "cooperating college" was frequently a misnomer. The proposal for a liaison person, appointed by the college to work with local school personnel, was considered essential in an effort to: 1) establish more harmonious relations between colleges and local schools, 2) bridge the gap between theory (advocated in college classrooms) and practice (employed in public school classrooms), and 3) assist elementary school teachers and administrators in upgrading reading instruction in the schools.

The results indicate that forty-four percent of the responding schools have accepted the recommendation. Much of this has been achieved as a result of field centered and onsite innovations in teacher education.

Where modifications of the recommendation are in effect, they usually refer to the appointment of faculty members on an informal basis—most frequently, directors of student teaching or supervisors of student teaching. Since these staff members can function as liaison persons only on a part-time basis, their services do not necessarily fulfill the intent of the recommendation. Once again budgetary considerations and time preclude more widespread acceptance of the recommendation.

Recommendation 17

That colleges encourage students to remain in local cooperating schools for a full day during the practice teaching program so that their understanding of the continuity of the reading program may be strengthened.

RESULTS

	N	%
1. in effect	128	79.
2. modified or strengthened	22	13.
3. not in effect	6	3.
4. not applicable	2	1.
5. no response	3	1.
	161	100.0

REPRESENTATIVE COMMENTS

"Required to have a full day experience for a full semester."

"The above is an absolute requirement for practice teaching."

"Students live in the community where student teaching occurs. They remain in the school one full semester and are in the school for the entire day."

"Full day as seniors; half day as juniors."

"Student teaching is a sixteen week full time, full day experience."

"State law requires this in our progam."

DISCUSSION

The original study stated that "slightly less than half of the colleges participating in the field study reported that their students were required to do only half-day student teaching during the apprenticeship program" (1:153). Because the staff felt that many prospective teachers were unable to observe or participate in the continuity of the reading program, when student teaching was either abbreviated and/or where reading was taught by the cooperating teacher at a time other than when student teachers were present in the classroom, the recommendation was made for full time student teaching.

Follow up results indicate that this recommendation is in effect in an overwhelming number of schools and represents a substantial change from fifteen years ago.

Recommendation 18

That not more than two students be assigned to practice teach simultaneously in one cooperating classroom.

RESULTS

	N	%
1. in effect	116	72.0
2. modified or strengthened	31	19.2
3. not in effect	8	5.0
4. not applicable	4	2.5
5. no response	2	1.2
	161	99.9

REPRESENTATIVE COMMENTS

"We allow only one student teacher to one cooperating teacher."

"Always have."

"Seldom do we have more than one unless there is a teaming arrangement."

"I laugh at this when I recall having six to eight in one class back in the 50s and 60s. Teachers will not permit more than one, and reluctantly so at that!"

"Policy is to assign not more than one student teacher per classroom except in a few experimental programs where a student teacher may be paired with a junior intern."

DISCUSSION

It is obvious, from the results, that this recommendation has been widely adopted. Even in those colleges where the respondent indicated that the recommendation was "not in effect," the accompanying comment was indicative of the fact that more than one student could be placed in a single cooperating classroom but usually for only a specific period of time. When the recommendation was not in effect, this almost always occurred in campus demonstration schools where space was limited. It should be noted that, since the first study was published, there has been a widespread decline in the use of campus schools for practice teaching and related purposes.

Recommendation 19

That where students are assigned to one classroom during practice teaching, provisions be made for them to participate in directed observation programs at other grade levels.

RESULTS

	N	%
1. in effect	106	65.8
2. modified or strengthened	33	20.5
3. not in effect	16	9.9
4. not applicable	4	2.5
5. no response	2	1.2
	161	99.9

REPRESENTATIVE COMMENTS

"Our students have two different grade level assignments."

"This is a logistical problem that the theoretician cannot possibly understand."

"This arrangement is made, but it varies from school to school."

"Since our students are in classrooms for a least a full year, this is not necessary for student teaching."

"Prior to student teaching our students have two quarters, twenty full days per quarter, of directed observation and participation."

"Required observation and miniteaching at several grade levels by most of our students."

"Probably done in 75 percent of the situations. Often at primary and intermediate levels."

"Sophomore year each student spends one-half day for the full semester in a school as a teacher assistant: eight weeks in a primary grade and eight weeks in an intermediate grade."

"In some locations, this occurs. We recommend it, although it is not implemented 100 percent."

"This varies from school to school."

DISCUSSION

When this recommendation was made, the staff was concerned with the future effectiveness of those prospective teachers who did their practice teaching at one level with no guarantee that they would subsequently be assigned a teaching position at that level. Field interviews with numerous graduated teachers confirmed this problem; many were unhappy to find themselves in an intermediate grade after experiencing a practice teaching role exclusively at the primary level, or vice versa.

Results of this study indicate that the recommendations for expanded experiences is in effect, and it has been strengthened in many colleges where student teaching is required at both the primary and intermediate grade levels.

Recommendation 20

That where the student is found to have specific weaknesses in understanding the total reading program, the student be required to return to the college, following practice teaching, for additional course work.

That where a student is weak in the area of instructional techniques, student apprenticeship be prolonged until a predetermined degree of competency is attained.

RESULTS[*]

	Part A		Part B	
	N	%	N	%
1. in effect	39	24.2	49	30.4
2. modified or strengthened	27	16.8	29	18.0
3. not in effect	80	49.7	70	43.5
4. not applicable	14	8.7	12	7.4
5. no response	1	0.6	1	0.6
	161	100.0	161	99.9

[*]See also Appendix C.

"A student who is found to have specific weaknesses is withdraw from student teaching for a semester."

"Competency program should help to implement these recommer dations."

"True in reading preparation but not in practice teaching."

"While this has been done, it has been mainly a desperation remedi ation gesture."

"In theory, this is fine; in reality, it usually is not done."

"This is not possible the way our program is structured."

"This is easy to recommend but hard to implement. We canno agree among ourselves on what proficiency entails."

"We recycle students and, in fact, counsel students out prior to an during student teaching."

"No such flexibility is now possible."

"The six hour reading block with practicum in the school has pre vented such specific weaknesses prior to student teaching. During student teaching???"

"Have not found this imperative to date."

"No such provisions are made, nor are provisions made for remedi ation."

"Students either pass or fail through performance based criteria."

"Students are asked to repeat part or all of the teaching period in the laboratory school if the degree of success in local schools is poor However, this expediency is rarely ever resorted to."

DISCUSSION

Just as the study staff was concerned with the criteria used to admit students to programs of teacher preparation, they also were concerned about exit requirements reflected in this recommenda tion. More specifically, while many of the respondents showed deep concern over the absence of individualized instruction in elementary school teaching situations, there appeared to be little transfer of this concern to college teaching classes. It was taken for granted that prospective teachers form a relatively homogeneous group and, as such, receive much the same instruction, fulfill the same tasks, and submit to the same exit requirements. Observations indicated that many students had the potential to complete the prescribed teacher preparatory program in the traditional four year period; however, some students could have profited from additional course work and a few students could have completed the program with less work.

The results of the present survey indicate that neither part of recommendation 20 is in effect in a majority of schools. In examining the comments, most respondents account for this situation on the basis that they are handicapped by the administrative structure within their respective schools which precludes flexibility in scheduling. Others point out that a "predetermined degree of competency" is still something of an unknown quantity. Compounding the dilemma is the problem of assessment which, in most instances, becomes highly subjective so that, in the final analysis, attainment of competency (which of itself means many things to many people) is determined through the eyes of the beholder. And, in the case of attainment in reading competency, the beholder is frequently someone other than the instructor of reading. As frequently cited throughout this report, because of the complications of the teacher preparation program there is a division of labor between those who evaluate the theoretical side of the coin and those who assess its practical application. It is often a case of the left hand not knowing what the right hand is doing or, more graphically, the reading professor not knowing what the apprentice is doing. Until this discrepancy is corrected, colleges will continue to grant degrees to some students who are not adequately prepared to cope with the awesome responsibilities involved in teaching children to become mature readers.

Recommendation 21

That colleges reexamine the criteria used to evaluate students during the practice teaching experience to ensure that a passing grade in practice teaching does, in fact, mean that the student has achieved the desired level of competency in teaching reading and other elementary grade skills.

RESULTS

	N	%
1. in effect	90	55.9
2. modified or strengthened	24	14.9
3. not in effect	39	24.2
4. not applicable	6	3.7
5. no response	2	1.2
	161	99.9

REPRESENTATIVE COMMENTS

"Hopefully!"

"Our evaluation system is still lacking."

"In a sense, partially."

"The college is in agreement with this measure, but I do not know how effectively the goal is achieved."

"This practice is carried out in all methods courses throughout all si quarters."

"We are continuously weeding out those nice students who will no become good teachers."

"More emphasis is being placed on competency achievement."

"This area can stand some examination."

"The decision as to the level of competency in teaching reading seems to rest almost totally with the cooperating teacher."

"We are starting a competency based program."

"Depends on college personnel assigned to supervise student teaching."

"Grade C is still looked upon in the marketplace as a failing grade."

DISCUSSION

If this recommendation is in effect to the extent indicated, i represents a substantial change from the original findings when i was noted that "rarely, if ever, are students allowed to fail the practice teaching experience" (1:156). This observation was made irrespective of the performance of the student.

There is some justification for believing that the respondent who completed the follow up questionnaire may not have been accurately informed about the competency level of the student teacher or the student teaching program. A question could be raised about the validity of the responses due to the fact that large numbers of respondents who indicated the recommendation was in effect then qualified their responses with comments such as "hopefully," "probably," or "mostly," leaving an impression that they may well have been whistling in the dark.

Similarly, the validity of other results may be subject to question. For example, the reading instructor (who invariably assumes responsibility for the completion of questionnaire information) does not usually assume responsibility for the supervision of student teachers and frequently is not familiar with the performance level of students. On the other hand, where the cooperating teacher is responsible for grading, failing marks in student teaching may be assigned infrequently because they generally are considered to be a reflection on the competency of the cooperating teacher, rather

han the student. In other instances, students are still permitted to
nroll in student teaching programs during their final college
emester. With graduation so close at hand, it is a rare faculty mem-
)er who has the courage to give failing grades.

For some colleges, there is the expressed hope that the weak-
1esses in existing assessment procedures for student teachers may be
)vercome with the perfection of competency based programs.

Recommendation 22

*That colleges establish a program to follow up their graduates with
a view toward determining to what extent preparation has been
adequate and what weaknesses, if any, exist in student training.*

RESULTS	N	%
1. in effect	66	41.0
2. modified or strengthened	34	21.1
3. not in effect	53	32.9
4. not applicable	6	3.7
5. no response	2	1.2
	161	99.9

REPRESENTATIVE COMMENTS

"We do this each year."

"We contact employers, supervising teachers, and graduates to gain
their opinions."

"Reports by students and their administrators helped to support
need for additional work in reading and the addition of the second
required course."

"Some minor research studies done in this area."

"Such follow up is now mandated by state regulations."

"Establishing as result of NCATE visitation."

"Because of geographic dispersion of students, only selective follow
up can be done effectively."

"We are talking about this, but little beyond a questionnaire has
been accomplished so far."

"We have done some follow up but are just now designing our programs to provide this feedback on a regular basis."

"We'd like to do so but our students are highly mobile following
certification."

"On paper but not in practice."

The importance of establishing a follow up program to determine the success of graduating students, as well as conducting some *post facto* assessment of the strengths and weaknesses of baccalaureate programs as indicated by beginning teachers, is a goal which would be supported by most educators. That it is not done to the extent one would consider desirable is also understandable, since one respondent after another indicated that one of the major drawbacks in implementing the recommendation was the mobility of graduates. Another problem concerned employment attrition of graduated students, mostly as a result of marriage and pregnancy. Therefore, in most instances, only modest efforts at postgraduation evaluation are undertaken and the respondents who checked column two clearly indicated that their check represented a "modification" as opposed to a "strengthening."

There were encouraging signs, however, most notably reported by several respondents who indicated that feedback from their graduating students had resulted in the addition of reading courses to their curriculum.

Recent Changes in Preparatory Programs

Part 2 of the questionnaire asked respondents to indicate those changes that had taken place in their instructional program during recent years. Replies were received from 131 (81.4%) of the 161 participating colleges. Fifty of the colleges were subsequently contacted and asked to give more detailed information about their programs. Results of this part of the study are outlined in Table 1.

It was evident from an examination of the responses that recent changes clearly fell into three broad categories: scope, conduct, and related activities.

Scope

INCREASE IN THE NUMBER OF READING COURSES.

During the fifteen years since the first study was published, giant steps have been taken in the expansion of reading courses being made available and/or required of present day students. In 1961, it was found that 3 percent of the colleges included in the study did not require any reading courses for prospective students and approximately half included reading as a part of a course in language arts (where instructional time averaged out to be approximately eight clock hours). Today, there is almost unanimous agreement among respondents (94.4 percent) that the class time devoted to reading instruction is equivalent to at least three semester hours of credit.

This variation between yesterday and today can be traced, in part, to the role being played by state legislatures. In 1961, only eleven states required course work in reading as a prerequisite for certification. In 1976, that figure had risen to thirty-two states requiring course work in reading for certification at the elementary school level and fifteen states having specific requirements in reading for some or all secondary school teachers. Some states (such as New York) require two reading courses for certification and, effective September 1, 1976, in Arizona all graduates from elementary and secondary education programs who apply for certification must have four and two courses respectively in "Reading Education."

It could justifiably be said, then, that many of the recent changes have been brought about by state certifying requirements rather than college requirements. Yet, numerous colleges now offer two or more courses which have resulted from a college commitment to the improvement of reading instruction rather than to a requirement for certification in that state.

An interesting combination of the two can be found in Arizona where, as noted, multiple reading courses were prescribed. However, the state did not set requirements on course hours or credits. Thus, theoretically, the participating universities could agree to give four one semester hour courses. However, the three state universities agreed to teach each course as a separate three semester credit unit, thereby requiring elementary undergraduates to complete twelve semester hours in reading education and secondary majors to complete six semester hours.

Regardless of which agency should receive the credit for increased hours of baccalaureate reading instruction, the fact remains that reading courses are available in greater numbers today than they were in the past decade.

Table 1

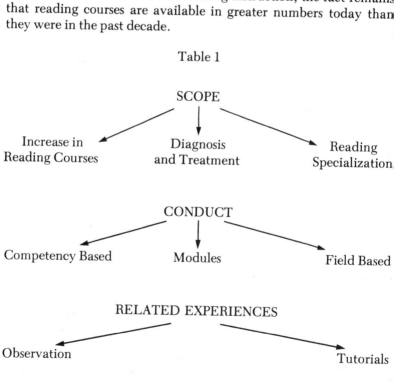

SCOPE

Increase in Reading Courses

Diagnosis and Treatment

Reading Specialization

CONDUCT

Competency Based

Modules

Field Based

RELATED EXPERIENCES

Observation

Tutorials

Considering the fact that in 1961 many college instructors were limited to less than eight hours of class time devoted to reading instruction, they were naturally frustrated in determining which topics should be included in the reading course and which topics would, of necessity, be eliminated. When instructors were asked to indicate which topics should receive more emphasis, if time were not a factor, diagnosis and treatment of reading disabilities headed their lists. At the same time, a majority of the reading instructors interviewed indicated that educational programs in the area of diagnosis and correction would be more appropriate at the graduate levels and, in particular, in the preparation of reading specialists. This point of view has apparently undergone some revised thinking since it is no longer unusual for colleges to offer undergraduate students a separate course in diagnosis and correction. This would appear to be eminently sensible if one believes in the principle that a good developmental reading program is a natural outgrowth of diagnosis and assessment of children's prevailing potential and achievement.

An examination of the topics receiving most emphasis in existing diagnosis and treatment classes includes:

> Basic principles of corrective reading
>
> Causes of reading underachievement
>
> The underachieving reader: Who is he?
>
> Survey of diagnostic instruments
>
> Assessment of diagnostic instruments
>
> Location of word analysis and comprehension difficulties
>
> Improving deficiencies in language, word analysis, comprehension, study skills, and content area reading

MAJORS, MINORS, AND SPECIALIZATION IN READING INSTRUCTION

Although programs leading to specialized concentration in reading instruction might have been in effect at the time of the original study, none were known to the staff. Indeed, the main effort behind *The Torch Lighters* was to increase the amount of time being devoted to reading instruction to the equivalent of at least three semester hour credits. Although present opportunity for specialization in reading instruction, to the extent of being considered a major or minor area of concentration, is not universally adopted it has become a reality in numerous colleges. Illustrations of three such programs follow:

A. Specialization in Reading (*minimum 26-27 semester hours*)
   Elementary

   Required Courses

Teaching of Reading in the Elementary School	(3)
Advanced Reading Techniques	(3)
Book Selection of Children and Young People	
or	
Children's Literature in Education	(3)
Teaching of Reading in the Secondary School	
or	
Reading in Early Childhood Education	(2-3)
Reading Disabilities	(3)
Reading Practicum	(3)

   Elective Courses (any three from the following)

Linguistic Approach to the Teaching of Reading	
Introduction to Linguistics	
Descriptive American-English Grammar	
Creative Drama	
Children's Theatre	
Keystones in Language	
Teaching English as a Second Language	
Educational Psychology of the Disadvantaged Urban Child	
Tests and Measurements	(9)

   Total 26-27

B. Specialization in Reading (*minimum 20 semester hours*)
   Elementary

   1. Knowledge of the Language (*minimum 8 semester hours*)

Introduction to Linguistics	(3)
Psychology of Reading	(3-4)
Methods: Elementary School Language Arts	(3)
Phonetics of American English	(3)
Children's Language Development	(3)
Introduction to Speech and Hearing Processes and Disorders	(3)

2. Methods and Materials (*minimum 3 semester hours*)

Methods: Elementary School Reading Clinical Experience	(3)
Reading Clinic: Teaching Techniques	(2)
and	
Reading Clinic: Teaching Practicum	(2-4)
or	
Supervised Teaching in Elementary School	arr.

3. Children's Literature (*minimum 3 semester hours*)

Children's Literature	(3)
Literature for Adolescents	(3)

4. Knowledge of the Child (*minimum 3 semester hours*)

The Learner	(3)
Socialization of the School-Age Child	(2-3)
Child Development	(3)
Adolescence	(3)
Cognitive Development of Children	(3)

C. Specialization in Reading (*24 semester hours*)

Secondary

Required Courses

Teaching Reading in the Junior and Senior High School	(3)
Problems in the Teaching of Reading	(3)
Linguistics and its Application to Reading Instruction	(3)
Teaching Reading in the Content Fields	(3)
Diagnostic and Remedial Reading	(3)
Practicum: Clinical Reading-Developmental	(3)
Practicum: Clinical Reading-Remedial	(3)
Literature for Young People	(3)

Conduct

In 1961, the expressions *competency based performance, modules,* and *field experiences* were terms practically unknown in reading circles. Today, they are commonplace. But to define them with any degree of accuracy becomes virtually impossible since each appears to have different meanings from one college to another.

Field experiences can be, and are, conducted in public school settings without reliance on modules or competency based programs. Modules can be completed apart from field experiences and without involving competency based performances. CBTE programs can be conducted without modules, although they almost always involve field experiences.

It is possible, also, for modules, CBTE, and field experiences all to be part of the same program. An example of the latter is cited from the correspondence of one respondent. When asked to elaborate on a statement that a modular approach to teaching represented a recent change in the school's instructional program, the respondent wrote in part:

> This statement reflects the undergraduate teacher education program in that each curriculum area is designed around a number of modules, some of which are required and some are not required. Students pursue the module in an independent study fashion with the aid of a professor or graduate teaching assistant. This aid is provided in a one to one teaching situation. Upon completion of each module, the student is evaluated by the graduate teaching assistant or the professor to determine whether the student has an adequate understanding of the module. A follow up to this evaluation is that the student goes to an elementary school to which the student had previously been assigned, teaches several aspects of the lesson from the module, and is evaluated by a supervising classroom teacher. Upon the completion of that evaluation, the student is given credit for having completed a module. This process is repeated a number of times in each of the curriculum areas, until the student has completed all of the modules in the entire undergraduate program.

Modules range in degree of complexity and sophistication from one college to another although, by and large, they tend to follow a similar format. The following module has been selected as a representative sample.

READING

MODULE B: Readiness for Beginning Reading Instruction*

Competencies

Upon completion of this module the student will be able to

1. Identify social, intellectual, physical, emotional, and educational factors related to reading readiness.
2. Describe home and school environmental influences on reading readiness.

---

*References to specific authors, tests, and textbooks have been deleted.

3. Distinguish between formal and informal measures of readiness.
4. Determine which children are ready to begin formal reading and which children need additional readiness activities.
5. Develop experiences and materials which enable children to develop specific readiness skills (auditory discrimination, visual discrimination, etc.).

Prerequisite

None.

Preassessment

Preassessment consists of alternative forms of the postassessment. See instructor.

Instructional Activities

Select from the following learning experiences those which you feel will enable you to achieve the competencies stated for this module.

1. Attend a seminar for orientation to this module.
2. Read one or more of the references on readiness for beginning reading. Use the following questions as your purposes for reading:
   a. What is the current view of the concept of "readiness for beginning reading"?
   b. What factors are identified as being related to readiness for reading (i.e., factors which contribute to success in beginning reading)? Do you find agreement among the references with regard to these factors?

   The following references are good sources of information for developing an understanding of readiness and the factors related to it: (cited)
3. One means of assessing a child's readiness for beginning reading is through the use of standardized reading readiness tests. The majority of these tests have only limited usefulness, however. Read one or more of the following references for an analysis of the limitations of standardized readiness tests:
                                 (cited)
4. While most readiness tests measure the same types of factors, there are a few tests that attempt to 1) measure a broader range of factors and 2) measure these factors in greater depth. Examine the specimen sets of the _____Tests and the_____

Tests. What factors are measured by the _____ Tests that are not measured by the_____Tests?

5. Even if a teacher uses a standardized readiness test, he will want to obtain additional information concerning each child using a variety of informal measures. Using the _____, and _____ and _____ references (both cited in activity #2) determine what informal measures a teacher may use in assessing readiness for reading.

6. Compare the Checklist for Reading Readiness and the Informal Readiness Inventory. In what ways are they alike? Different? Do you prefer one to the other? Is there a way in which you could take parts of each and combine them to develop another inventory?

7. Included in each basal reading series (a set of books and related materials designed to be used for teaching reading skills at successive levels of development) is a workbook or set of activities for developing readiness skills. Each workbook focuses on the sequential development of those specific skills needed for successful beginning reading in the series to which it belongs. Examine the readiness workbooks and materials in several basal reading series (e.g., those published by _____, _____, or _____). What common elements do you find? Are certain skills emphasized more in one workbook than in another? Select one skill (e.g., visual discrimination) and follow its sequential development throughout the workbook.

8. Much of the readiness program consists of materials and activities developed by the teacher. Develop a lesson for teaching a specific readiness skill and use it with a group of children or peers. If you use a group of peers, ask each one to complete the Peer Teaching Evaluation Form. The following references are excellent sources of ideas for activities:

(cited)

9. Read the case studies in the two references listed below.

(cited)

Note how the teachers make use of all the available information as they assess children's readiness for beginning reading instruction.

10. Arrange a conference with the instructor to discuss questions or problems related to this module.

11. Design your own activities.

A. Knowledge Level

1. Identify one factor related to readiness for beginning reading in each of the following categories: social, intellectual, physical, emotional, and educational. Performance is successful if each factor is correctly identified with the appropriate category.

2. Describe two ways in which the child's home and school environments each affect readiness for beginning reading. Performance is successful if the relationship between the home and school environmental influences and readiness for reading is clearly demonstrated.

3. Identify two ways in which formal and informal measures of readiness differ. Give one example of a formal measure and one example of an informal measure. Performance is successful if a) formal and informal measures of readiness are accurately differentiated and b) both examples given are correct.

4. Read the three case studies which will be provided for this posttest. Each one provides information concerning the background and development of one child. Decide for each child whether he is ready to begin reading instruction or needs additional readiness activities. State the reasons for your decisions. Performance is successful if a) each decision is defensible and b) the reasons given adequately support each decision.

B. Performance Level

1. Plan two activities which will contribute to the development of two specific skills (auditory discrimination, visual discrimination, language development, left-to-right orientation, etc.). Develop your own materials for these activities. Criteria for successful performance:

    a. Objectives state desired behavior

    b. Activities/materials are appropriate for the development of the specific skills identified

    c. Instructional steps described are in a defensible sequence

    d. Procedures for evaluation of pupil achievement are described

2. Arrange to teach the lessons to groups of two or more chil dren. Arrange to a) have the instructor or cooperating teacher observe one of the lessons or b) tape one of the lessons.

3. After you have taught the lessons, write lesson evaluation indicating a) to what extent pupils achieved objectives, b) what could be done to help pupils who did not achieve ob jectives, c) what problems were encountered, if any, and d) what type of follow up activity might provide useful practice at another time.

4. Follow one of these procedures:
   a. If instructor has observed lesson, schedule a conference to discuss plan and lesson
   b. If cooperating teacher has observed lesson, ask for writ ten evaluation and then schedule a conference with in structor to discuss plan, lesson, and, cooperating teach er's evaluation
   c. If lesson has been taped, schedule conference with in structor to discuss plan and tape

   Criteria for successful performance:
   a. There is evidence that pupils have achieved the objective
   b. Student has demonstrated the ability to adapt his teach ing strategy, as necessary, in response to pupil needs during lesson

References: Readiness for Beginning Reading Instruction
(cited)

In another CBTE program, competencies are divided into eight components with each component designed to measure a different facet of reading. Examples of an activity within each component follow:

Component 1 (Background)

Example   The student will develop in written form his/her philosophy of the reading process and the teach ing of reading.

Component 2 (Demonstration and Practice)

Example   The student will prepare, administer, and score teacher-made tests in the following areas: phonics, structural analysis, and context clues.

Component 3 (Research and Development)

Example   The student will prepare a minimum of ten games for implementing instruction, with at least two each in the following areas: sight words, structural analysis, comprehension, phonic analysis, and readiness.

Component 4 (Application)

Example   The student will submit a written preliminary report based on diagnosis, outlining the reading program to meet the specific needs of an individual student being tutored.

Component 5 (Theory)

Example   The student will demonstrate a thorough knowledge of developmental reading skills by helping in the construction of a developmental reading skills checklist.

Component 6 (Laboratory Experiences)

Example   The student will participate in the construction of an informal reading inventory.

Component 7 (Modules)

Example   The student will administer and interpret tests to check the following prereading skills: auditory discrimination, visual discrimination, and letter names.

Component 8 (Tutoring)

Example   The student will group and teach pupils in accordance with specific needs (minimum of sixteen one-hour teaching sessions). The student will complete the following:

    a. Select and utilize commercial instructional materials for the specific reading level of children within the given group

    b. Develop and utilize skill worksheets and instructional devices to meet specific needs

    c. Submit lesson plans for each teaching session, indicating goals and materials and procedures to be used

    d. Design, administer, and evaluate a reading lesson applicable to a specific content area

    e. Keep a written record of the progress of each student throughout the entire teaching period

After completion of each component, the student returns the necessary material for evaluation to the reading faculty member with whom he is working.

Just how successful these and other programs have been in increasing student understanding and performance is unknown at this time; although respondents were asked to evaluate the effectiveness of innovations cited, very few actually did. One respondent did describe the program briefly and then added a personal assessment

> The content of the course is divided into eight units such as approaches to reading instruction, word identification, readiness for initial reading, etc. Each unit is divided into competencies which the student should attain as a result of study; each competency is divided into behavioral objectives which relate to each competency; each behavioral objective has listed learning activities to be carried out. Learning activities may involve textual study, observations, examination of materials, etc. A study guide which the students purchase contains all of the above in outline form. A book of readings containing textual materials was also prepared to save students library time. The book of readings is purchased by each student, along with the study guide.

> Though this study guide seems to add structure to the programs by spelling out the objectives in more concrete form, I frankly cannot seem to see much change in students' overall level of understanding.

One additional change initiated by one of the responding colleges describes a required twenty-four clock hour "clinical experience" which is an addition to the usual requirements for a three semester hour foundations reading course. The experience is field based and is guided and evaluated by the supervising teachers. The clinical experience is divided into five parts:

Part I   Observation (four hours)

Visit several classrooms. For each classroom, list basal, supplementary materials, number of reading groups, and describe the teaching and management techniques being utilized.

Part II   Assessment and Prescription (five hours)

You are now assigned to one classroom and will be assigned to a small group of children. Following the directions of your supervising teacher you are to ascertain the specific reading needs of each child in your group. Second, you are to prescribe an instructional program for each child. For purposes of this journal, you are to enter a detailed description of your assessment and prescription for each child.

arts III and IV   Instruction (ten hours)

During this ten hour period you are to instruct the children in your group. Enter detailed descriptions of the instructional periods to include the following: extent of individualization, basal, supplementary materials and activities, management techniques, and copies of several lesson plans.

art V   Evaluation (five hours)

During this period you are to evaluate your children's progress as directed by your supervising teacher. From this evaluation you are to reassess the instructional needs and represcribe instructional materials for each of your children. For purposes of this journal, describe this five hour period by entering a detailed description of your evaluation, reassessment, and represcription for each child.

Related Experiences

In noting recent changes in their teacher education programs, numerous schools cited observation and tutorial programs as related or integrated aspects of the reading course. The earliest involvement by the prospective teacher is at the freshman year where students participate as observers in elementary and junior high classrooms. Such involvement is more typical, however, at the sophomore and junior levels. A capsule version of one new program which utilizes observations and tutorial teaching is included here:

Sophomore Year

Students serve as teacher aides six hours per week for sixteen weeks.

Junior Year

Students spend one-half day per week, for sixteen weeks, in an elementary classroom during a Human Development course. They complete a case study on one child and perform limited instructional tasks.

Students take the language arts, math, reading, science, and social studies methods courses taught by a team of professors. Students spend two days per week, for sixteen weeks, in classrooms performing teaching activities related to each of the methods courses and assisting teachers in other ways.

Senior Year

Student teaching for twelve weeks.

Since considerable emphasis is placed on student observation and student-pupil interaction at these colleges, as well as many others, we compiled a list of observations to be made as well as a list of those activities which baccalaureate students are most frequently asked to complete:

Observation Guide

1. Physical characteristics of the classroom
    seating arrangement
    composition of display boards
    other classroom displays
    chalkboard space utilization

2. Likenesses and differences in pupil characteristics
    chronology   race
    sex   general appearance

3. Availability and kinds of reading materials
    reading texts   magazines
    library books   audiovisual materials

4. Predominant mode of instruction
    individual
    small group
    whole class

5. Teaching techniques used when pupils cannot decode or recognize words.

6. Teaching techniques used when pupils are being evaluated on their comprehension abilities.

7. Motivation techniques used by the teacher.

8. Forms of encouragement/reinforcement utilized by the teacher

9. Relation of reading instruction to other classroom activities.

10. Extent of pupil mobility.

Activity Guide

1. Select a library book and read it to a small group of children. Note:

    Did the story hold the interest of the children?

    To what extent did the children interact in a follow up discussion?

    Do you think the story was too short, too long, just right?

. Select a picture from a magazine or book that will presumably motivate children in a discussion of its contents. Show the picture to children individually and ask:

"What do you think is happening in this picture?"

Show the same picture to several children and note:

How did language skills of children differ?

Did boys respond differently than girls?

Did older children respond differently from young children?

. Administer any of the following tests that are appropriate to the achievement level of your class:

reading readiness checklist

phonics inventory

interest inventory

attitude inventory

. Select one child to observe. Within a twenty minute period, make a notation every thirty seconds of what the child is doing.

. Observe one teacher for a thirty minute period. At one minute intervals, record what the teacher is doing.

. Using the adaptations you have made from the _____ book, indicate the outcome of the activities used in terms of your stated objectives.

. Note similarities and differences between the theory expressed in class lectures and practices observed in the schools. This should refer primarily to the teaching of reading/language arts.

. Compile a list of questions you would like your instructor to answer when you return to resume your lectures (these should relate primarily to the teaching of reading and arise from your observations and related reading).

In summary, the most recent changes, or those in the process of hanging, include increased numbers of reading courses and a move om offering instruction on campus to field based schools where udents are more likely to engage in competency based instruction. nd more schools are expanding their professional sequence from e traditional junior and senior years down to the freshman and phomore levels.

Chapter 3

Respondents' Recommendations

Although 81 percent of the respondents completed Part 2 of the questionnaire, slightly less than half (45.3 percent) completed Part in which the respondent was asked to indicate recommendations to improve preparatory programs. This significant drop in the number of replies may indicate one of two things: either most of the respondents were satisfied with their existing programs or they encountered a problem of fatigue after completing a long and difficult questionnaire. We like to think it was the latter.

An analysis of the eighty-eight responses provided in Part indicates that these recommendations fall into several logical categories: scope, related reading experiences, course conduct, content, student teaching, inservice education, support, and student/faculty quality. Each of these areas will be considered.

Scope

The most predominant recommendation among the respondents was that prospective secondary school teachers be required to complete a course in the teaching of reading. This recommendation was made in the original study and, as reported in Chapter 2, has now been implemented by a majority of colleges of education. Two representative comments follow:

> All preservice secondary teachers need *at least* one course in reading.

> While recommendation 9 from *The Torch Lighters* urged that a course in basic reading instruction be required for all secondary school teachers, this practice has not become part of secondary programs at our university. This appears to be reflected in a large proportion of colleges and universities across the nation. This recommendation should be given specific attention and emphasis in the near future. It seems most important that the college faculty responsible for this component of secondary teacher education have strong preparation in reading education (as well as subject area strength) so that the balance between process of reading and content can be

understood by students and subsequently applied in a meaningful way in their classrooms. Conflicts in the perception of teachers' roles relative to process and content have long been a deterrent in implementation of effective reading programs at advanced levels.

A related recommendation was for more required reading courses for prospective elementary school teachers. These recommendations ranged from "more than one" course to twelve semester hours of required study. One respondent would program the second course *after* student teaching:

In this course, students should get information and competence in: administering an individual diagnostic reading test and using the findings to provide appropriate reading experiences; selecting various types of instructional materials to meet differences in pupils' interests and reading skill needs; learning how to teach *successfully* children *within* the classroom who are moving at a slow pace; and using observation of pupil behavior in evaluating performance rather than relying exclusively upon test results.

This concern with diagnosis was also expressed by numerous other respondents who felt the need for a course in that particular phase of reading:

Recommendation for skill in using a diagnostic approach to reading instruction beginning with the prekindergarten child.

Diagnostic instruction for the classroom teacher is a must for future instruction. A greater proportion of underachieving readers can be expected due to increased incidence of auditory perceptual problems, increased number of disadvantaged pupils, and increasing extent of urbanization.

Related Reading Experiences

Much support was shown for earlier student involvement with pupils, for a practicum related to the basic reading course, and for guided field experiences.

Involve students in an early and continuous plan for working with children throughout the four year experience, focusing on minilessons in tutoring, small group instruction, and specific skills development.

Continue experimentation with proper mixture and sequence of laboratory experiences and classroom theory.

Tie in a field based experience with courses in reading.

In the past, we have been sending students on observation a[n] tutorial expeditions without any supervision of their efforts. W[e] could be doing them a disservice rather than a service. Wh[at] we recommend is more carefully controlled and *guided* supe[r] vision in these required experiences related to reading i[n] struction.

Course Conduct

Two of the controversial issues of the time—the development [of] modules and competency based performance—dominated t[he] recommendations for changing the evaluation of teaching and a[s] sessing the fundamental and subsequent courses in reading. Modul[es] were suggested for almost every known component of reading an[d] advocates of competency based programs outnumbered their d[e] tractors by about four to one. This ratio is reflected in some repr[e] sentative comments included below:

An even greater emphasis on field based programs, using com[ ] petency based criteria for the evaluation of reading skills.

Development of competency based programs in some form.

CBTE recommended.

We can only see a brighter future for reading instructio[n] through some form of competency based instruction. It doesn['t] make sense that I grade students A, B, C, D, F in a cours[e] called "The Teaching of Reading" when I don't know wheth[er] they *can* teach reading.

Recommended that competency based instruction, as a mea[ns] to evaluate success in teacher preparation, be given a dece[nt] burial.

Recommendations directed toward the conduct of reading in[ ] struction were not exclusively related to CBTE. Several recommenda[ ] tions related to the use of microteaching and videotaping. One suc[h] technique used with prospective secondary students is outlined be[ ] low:

We recommend an approach that we have found successfu[l] Two professors use videotaping with microteaching in [ ] secondary general methods course with emphasis on such fe[a] tures as motivation, variation of stimuli, reinforcement, cl[o] sure, and questioning techniques. These students have special[i] zations in areas such as English and social studies and are bein[g] certified. After each videotaping experience, the instructor con[ ] ducts a counseling-critiquing session with the student while r[e] viewing the videotape.

uring the late 50s and early 60s the major controversy in reading rcles related to the who, what, where, when, and why of phonic alysis and several recommendations in *The Torch Lighters* atmpted to deal with the problem. Today it appears to be a dead sue, at least to the extent that respondents failed to mention it in eir recommendations relating to course content. What they did ress was more attention to language development, linguistics, and alect:

Future programs should recognize that reading is an integral part of language development and the acquisition of literacy and, therefore, that professors should provide students the opportunity to gain some modern concepts of language acquisition.

Require one course in the structure of language prior to professional courses in reading.

Increased attention to linguistics, psycholinguistics, and dialect as they are related to the reading process.

Solid grounding in linguistics, developmental reading and language arts, and children's literature.

Understanding of child growth and developmental patterns as also urged by numerous respondents:

Give students a thorough grounding in child development and implications it has for the teaching of reading.

Instructors should recognize that methods of reading instruction reflect implicit, if not explicit, concepts of children, learning, and the purpose of reading. (Undergraduate students are often exposed to an array of methods before they have developed any criteria for judging the underlying assumptions of the methods.)

I would strongly urge: 1) more emphasis upon analysis of learning characteristics of individual children, 2) understanding of the theoretical basis of variant instructional programs and teaching procedures, and 3) a reconciliation of 1 and 2.

The end result would be (hopefully) the selection of instructional procedures and materials on the basis of known characteristics of specific children rather than on the basis of a generalized notion of what should constitute the instructional program. This will require, among other things, a thorough understanding of the communication process.

Some of these latter recommendations were closely linked still another—that college instructors need to pay more attention the theory of reading and less attention to skill teaching.

It is regrettable that so many of our students are engaged in or miss activities when more often than not they have on minimal understanding of the "why" of what it is they a doing. If the present theme in public schools is "back to basic we have to begin with some theoretical basis, and I am afra that too many of our students are not receiving this kind of i struction.

More attention should be directed to understanding the lear ing modalities of children. Just as we came to the understan ing that there was no one set of instructional materials th would be equally good for all children, so, too, should we i culcate in the minds of our pupils the understanding that th bag of tricks often used in tutorial programs may not be a propriate for all children.

The topic of reading materials and visual aids was a major co cern of many respondents.

Opportunities to see, handle, and try out varied materials ar procedures in reading seem to have real value for learners. E panding the availability of reading resource centers and cc lections of materials is recommended for teacher education pr grams.

More and better resource materials and media.

That teacher preparation programs provide opportunities fe undergraduates to use a wide variety of textual and audiovisu materials that are used to teach reading in the schools.

That a lab center be established in conjunction with the audie visual department for the purpose of assisting students in th development of their own teaching materials.

Finally, a number of respondents felt that an attempt should l made to separate the numerous approaches to teaching beginnin reading from those needed for reading instruction in the middle an upper grades. These respondents were recommending two discree reading courses.

Student Teaching

Some weak links in the teacher education program would appear t be selected aspects of the student teaching program, including th es of cooperating teachers, the reading instructor, and the dent teaching supervisor. Yet, few of the respondents included ommendations dealing with these problem areas. The most likely planation is that respondents to the questionnaire were inevitably ading instructors and, as such, were not aware of many of the ortcomings surrounding student teaching programs since, more ely than not, they were removed from related student teaching tivities. Respondents who chose to deal with the issue made these ommendations:

Require a heavy emphasis in actually *teaching* reading during student teaching versus doing an integrated "core" sort of thing.

During supervision of student teaching, faculty from reading department assist supervising teachers in primary and elementary classes.

A full year of internship in the schools that would involve both student teaching activities and a number of methods courses.

During and after student teaching, every pupil should serve as an apprentice or aide to a reading consultant.

Regular contacts are required within a college on a secheduled basis between staff members who teach and those who supervise student teachers. Regularly scheduled meetings between coordinators, administrators, and staff are required for frank and open expression of concerns based upon formal and informal assessment of programs. Too often, college staffs assess only once every several years and then it is done under the duress of an accreditation review.

Unless we can attract teachers who are "masters" in fact, as well as in name, student teaching will remain what it is—a disaster.

service Education

ne does not normally think of inservice education as a component art of prospective teacher education although, presumably, there a peripheral element of inservice education during contacts that assroom teachers must have with their college students during torial, observation, and student teaching programs, as well as the le teachers fulfill in field based instruction. Consequently, several commendations were made that relate to inservice education.

Greater effort on the part of colleges to help local authorities build a strong inservice program in reading.

We recommend an exchange program between the college and the local schools including mutually exchanged observation opportunities for students and inservice teachers to exchange opinions and ideas about reading, and much more social contact. In this way, we think we can be of service in improving our own preparatory program as well as influencing inservice education.

In the limited time available, colleges can only prepare short order cooks who follow recipes. In order for the cooks to become chefs, we recommend a follow up program in which our reading professors join our graduates in the kitchen in the hope that the souffles will not fall.

Support

One of the high service words used frequently throughout the questionnaire returns was *more*; more reading courses, more faculty, more materials, and (not unexpectedly) more money. The following recommendations reflect some of this financial thinking:

We would recommend greater funding to provide larger facilities with more equipment to reach a larger number of teacher education students. If foundation money were available for plant expansion and audiovisual equipment, services to prospective reading students could be enhanced.

Financial support of students and private universities.

Higher education has a contemptuous fiscal attitude toward the financing of teacher education programs when compared with science programs. Our recommendation would be to reverse this priority.

And something of a reverse:

Rescind funds, both federal and state, when school systems do not employ teachers who meet the reading certification requirements established by their graduating institution.

Student/Faculty Quality

While respondents expressed continued concern over the quality of students, the recognition that the faculty may evidence some specific weaknesses was also expressed in recommendations made to overcome such problems. (The staff cannot recall any such concern about weaknesses of college instructors during the initial study

me representative recommendations are included below in direct
tio to those received.

That your recommendation number 1 be reemphasized. Quality in teachers is important, but it is difficult to arrive at that quality when you do not start with a quality product.

Recommend that faculty employed to teach reading to pre-service teachers be prepared academically and personally to understand the setting where most graduating students will be employed, which by no stretch of the imagination will be in reading clinics.

More minority group faculty who understand the reading problems associated with children labeled as minority group pupils. Our reading instructors are totally divorced from the realities of the child in the urban school.

An outstanding staff of professors who are research oriented as well as practical is urgently needed. This problem is circular. Institutions with poor staffs in reading must commit themselves absolutely to inservice development or a procedure of non-reward for staffs that do not grow, as well as meticulous searches for new faculty with high promise. Institutions with outstanding staffs (a rare few) must be prepared to offer every degree of stimulation and reward to hold the staff and enhance the conditions for service.

We recommend that instructors demonstrate excellence in the understanding and application of the reading process and that they not be merely language arts generalists.

In reviewing the recommendations of the respondents, it is evi-ent that many are the concern of their immediate college and not ecessarily applicable to other teacher preparatory settings. Recom-endations for more than one required course in reading, for xample, are already in effect at many colleges. Other recommen-ations, such as the one requiring a course in basic reading for econdary teachers, were made in the original study (and can be con-dered as germane today as fifteen years ago). Still other recom-endations would seem to merit consideration by all teacher reparatory schools—in particular, those recommendations dealing ith student teaching, course content, and faculty quality.

Chapter 4

Model Programs

Chapter 2 clearly shows the extent of interest in competency based education for prospective teachers. The momentum toward CBTE such that by 1976, more than one-third of the nation's states ha mandated CBTE programs, either as the only route to teacher certi cation or as a viable alternative to conventional plans. To educato already familiar with the movement toward greater accountabilit CBTE represents a possible strategy for maximizing the correspon ence between what teachers learn in collegiate courses and how the actually perform in classrooms. Hopefully, in the process, the pre verbial gap between theory and practice will be lessened cor siderably, if not closed permanently.

The description of a teacher education program in reading a College A illustrates a competency based alternative for the sing required reading course at that institution.

COLLEGE A—Competency Based Model

Type	State Supported, general college, coeducation.
Setting	New England, metropolitan
Enrollment	Approximately 5,000 undergraduates, 3,000 full- and part-time graduates

INSTRUCTIONAL MODULES

College A introduced a completely revised curriculum for unde graduates in 1970, including an innovative general studies progra for all students. Beginning in 1973, its department of education im plemented a competency based alternative for the required thre credit course in Methods and Materials in Teaching Reading. B 1976, this new section for undergraduates in elementary educatio had grown from a pilot project with ten volunteer students and on instructor to a project with sixty students and two instructors During the intervening period when the project was being fiel

sted and revised, the staff wrote a special 200 page student *Handbook* containing fourteen modular topics generally arranged in
erarchial order. All students were expected to complete the required objectives within the first nine modules. The remaining
topics could be selected when the "required" objectives had been
tained. The final list of instructional modules included (6):

1. Stating Behavioral Objectives in Reading
2. Nature of the Reading Process
3. Assessing Performance in Reading
4. Reading Readiness
5. Basal Reader
6. Word Identification
7. Comprehension
8. Language Experience Approach
9. Individualized Reading
10. Additional Approaches to Reading Instruction
11. Work-Study Skills
12. School and Classroom Organization for Individualizing
    Instruction
13. Readability
14. Children with Reading Difficulties

The objectives determined for the fourteen modules eventually
numbered fifty-four, with a minimum of twenty-five to be completed by the end of the semester (grades are partly based on the
number of objectives mastered). Usually, these objectives range from
cognitive competencies to those involving experiences with children.
Extracting an example from Developing Comprehension Skills, we
find the following (6):

1. The student will demonstrate an understanding of the different types of comprehension and the specific types of
   skills that apply to each level—literal, interpretive, critical.

2. The student will demonstrate the teaching of a specific
   comprehension skill by planning and implementing a lesson with a group of children.

The above objectives are required. Those below are optional:

1. The student will review a workbook, kit, audiotape, or
   programed material which can be used for the teaching of
   one or more comprehension skills.

2. The student will prepare teacher-made material that can
   be used in a lesson for teaching a specific comprehension
   skill.

3. The student will develop a lesson plan that demonstrat[es] the teaching of a comprehension skill (other than the o[ne] demonstrated in Requirement 2).

4. The student will develop an annotated bibliography th[at] includes brief descriptions of three commercial materia[ls] which can be used to develop skills in comprehension.

Gradually, a standard format of three parts emerged for eac[h] module: 1) a cover page which introduced the module, 2) lists [of] objectives with accompanying learning activities and techniques f[or] postassessment, and 3) related materials to be used with the modul[e]. As the staff extended various modular components, the choice [of] learning activities and postassessment techniques expanded als[o]. Suggested learning activities, for example, might include: profe[s]sional readings, live or videotaped lectures, seminars and grou[p] discussions, individual conferences, live demonstrations or demo[n]strations on videotape or audiotape, manipulation of material[,] films and filmstrips, and experiences with children. Equally varie[d] postassessments could be chosen from among those that involve[e] writing papers, taking objective or short essay tests, working wit[h] instructional materials and media to complete task analysis sheet[s] preparing projects related to the objectives of the module, or bein[g] observed during specific teaching situations.

MANAGEMENT SYSTEM

A successful competency based program appears to depend, in larg[e] measure, upon a well-developed management system—the pla[n] whereby students enter the program, get involved in learnin[g] activities, and either continue in the program or leave it. The syste[m] also specifies how faculty time and instructional resources will b[e] utilized. Admittedly, some faculties have overlooked or mishandle[d] this important component, perhaps through concern for other fea[t]tures of CBTE.

In planning a management system, the staff of College A face[d] the reality that its students had had little or no previous experienc[e] with competency based instruction. Therefore, the *Handboo[k]* which contained the modules and the accompanying printed ma[t]terial for the course became required student purchases. The firs[t] module serves as an orientation to the nature and characteristics o[f] competency based instruction and how it differs from conventiona[l] counterparts. The staff "walked" students through the introductor[y]

it and arranged to meet weekly with the entire class for the pur-
se of introducing new modules, resolving individual and group
oblems, scheduling small group discussions, and clarifying any
estions about the management system.

Because critics of modular designed courses have pointed to the
ngers of mechanized and dehumanized approaches to education,
llege A took special precautions to ensure that its management
tem established practical procedures for open student/faculty in-
actions on a regular basis. These opportunities included (6):

1. Required attendance at the weekly orientation sessions re-
   ferred to above.

2. A procedure for scheduling time with the instructor. For
   this, a student/instructor scheduling form was posted for
   use by students in arranging individual and group sessions with the instructor.

3. A way of scheduling activities with resource teachers at the
   field-site schools. Students used this procedure whenever
   they wanted to be observed as they implemented lessons
   with groups of children or to administer a reading test. It
   enabled them to make appointments with reading resource
   teachers for the teaching or testing experiences.

A third feature of the management system at College A related
the monitoring of student progress in the course. For each ob-
ctive attempted, students submitted a form to indicate their
oices. When they accomplished the objectives, the completed
rms were placed in individual student folders as records of their
ork. Progress was also displayed on a huge graph located in the
eading Center. As students completed objectives, dates were
ritten in appropriate spaces after their names. The graph provided
udents and staff with a rapid review of progress at any given time.

Each instructional module contains a list of learning activities
 facilitators of the objectives. Providing materials to implement
ese learning activities often becomes a formidable task, as many
olleges will testify. As a fourth part of its management system, Col-
ge A planned that students would have easy access to materials
sted in the *Handbook*. The college library placed a collection of
rofessional texts and journal articles on reserve; examples of in-
ructional materials in reading were made available in the college
urriculum center; and professional readings and instructional ma-
erials were placed in the field-site schools. Commercially prepared
acher education materials were purchased and used (primarily

during the early stages of program development) but, as the program progressed, it became essential to prepare demonstration lessons and lecture presentations on video- and audiotape. Locally designed instructional materials, found to be more relevant than many commercially prepared items, were housed in the Reading Center for use by students in CBTE.

Program Evaluations

As prospective teachers complete the competency based Methods and Materials in Reading course, they are asked to respond to a questionnaire dealing with their experiences. Some items call for decisions about the theory of CBE and student ability to pace their work during the semester. Most students agree with the theories of individualized instruction and self-pacing, although many are only partially satisied with their ability to pace themselves. They indicate that their productivity increases, often dramatically, in direct relationship to established deadlines for the course (there are two). At least two reasons may account for the admitted lack of satisfaction in self-pacing: course work may have been more demanding than anticipated and, in their first competency based course, students may have found the self-discipline required for pacing themselves in need of further development.

When trainees rate both the required and the optional modules as to effectiveness in helping them become teachers of reading, they place Reading Readiness and Children with Learning Difficulties at the top. Both modules call for experiences with children, especially valued activities for beginning teachers as confirmed by the group's high rating given to this item as the most effective learning technique. Reading of professional literature, individual student-professor conferences, and small group seminars also received favorable recognition as helpful learning activities.

As judged by students, the most effective types of postassessment are formal observations of lessons they have taught children and the construction of projects. These undergraduates obviously consider involvement with children as highly desirable, whether as a learning experience or as a postassessment option.

Course participants also answer questions about the process of CBTE. Almost without exception, participants respond that a competency based course requires more work than a conventional one; they also rate it as being more valuable. Despite these convictions, a rge majority find it difficult to commit themselves to another mpetency based course, should it be made available to them.

iscussion

uring the early 1970s, colleges undertaking CBTE found themselves ruggling with the identification of myriads of tentative teacher mpetencies, the preparation of instructional materials and evalu- ion procedures, and the validation of the new teacher education rriculum. Although little help was available for these pioneers, ost experienced educators believed they could recognize good aching when they observed it and, consequently, it should be no big thing" to produce a list of desired competencies. In the first days f developing such lists, participants of *The Torch Lighters Revisted* ppear to have followed one or two common routes. One possibility cused upon the efforts of a consortium of university and public hool people working together until they could state and agree pon the competencies to be developed. The consortium then ssembled groups of professional personnel to validate the com- etencies they had identified. A second route to the listing of in- tructional behaviors was exemplified by North Carolina which ormed ad hoc committees, each assigned to one certification area. he committees worked for two years before presenting their results o the state board of education. North Carolina now provides a state atalogue of competencies and suggested program guidelines to help nstitutions in developing teacher preparation programs. It should e noted that these competencies are stated in broad, general terms rom which specific subcompetencies must be generated by the col- eges planning to use them.

By whatever approach institutions choose to identify teaching ompetencies, it is no longer necessary to "reinvent the wheel." Granted that the delineation of discrete behaviors is far more dif- icult and time consuming than most people realize, a vast pool tands ready for use today—no small accomplishment in itself. There is, however, great need to establish priorities for varying ircumstances and settings. How can modifications of existing state- nents be made on the basis of the changing needs of schools and on he strengths and weaknesses of individual teacher trainees? These questions, and others, deserve scrutiny as colleges and universities attempt to reach goals in teacher preparation by means of com- etency based education programs.

Few beginners in the implementation of competency base programs anticipated the challenging frustrations in accomplishing the next steps of CBTE. Those who did made early decisions regarding how much of a course to modularize for an initial trial. College A, for example, inserted modules in the second half of its reading course, realizing that instructors required time to develop drafts of additional modules, gather materials for learning activities, and organize field sites for experiences with children. These and other components were completed in subsequent semesters, subject to testing and revision.

Throughout the country, competency based programs introduce modular units which vary greatly in organization, content and length. In some universities, although the traditional reading methods course remains in the undergraduate catalog, instructional modules provide flexibility and individualization within the course. Students at Ball State University who opt the new Right to Read teacher preservice program (Project LARC) enroll for one year in a competency based, block program for which they receive credit for four courses offered in the regular curriculum: Language Arts in the Lower Elementary Grades, Teaching of Reading in the Elementary School, Principles of Teaching and Classroom Management, and Corrective Reading. LARC students progress at their own rate through a series of instructional units, each designed to include clusters of knowledge or related critical skill competencies in reading instruction. Individualized Content Block I, for example, contains three clusters: understanding the nature of the English language, understanding the nature of language development in children, and understanding the content of language arts.

At George Peabody College for Teachers, the use of modular instructional units has increased in four revised courses: Reading in the Elementary School, The Improvement of Reading, Individualizing Language Arts Instruction in the Elementary School, and Procedures in Remedial Reading. Teaching assistants often work with Peabody students in the completion of modules, freeing the faculty to coordinate a heavier emphasis upon practicum experiences for prospective teachers.

Many college faculties in reading prefer to develop their own instructional modules. Some start with those used in other college programs, modifying them in accordance with their facilities and student needs, while staff efforts are directed toward the construction of additional modules. One of the best sources of resource and

tructional modules is the International Reading Association's
blication, *Modular Preparation for Teaching Reading* (5), a
oduct of the work of the IRA Commission on High Quality Teacher
lucation. The Commission will publish additional modules in the
ture.

Innovative teacher education programs of the 1970s may be
aracterized by multimedia instructional processes in conjunction
th high frequency opportunities for self-instruction. Students
ten request, but seldom find, videotaped "model performances" of
aching skills in reading, particularly those which cannot be
sualized easily from printed descriptions.

To what extent CBTE has advanced the cause of multimedia is
obably unknown, but for several years teacher education pro-
ams have utilized instructional technology to improve classroom
aching and learning. Videotape feedback, for instance, continues
be of specific interest as a means of changing preservice and in-
rvice teacher behaviors. Studies of teacher reactions to video play-
ack appear to indicate that, while discrepant feedback can be dis-
rbing to individuals, self-viewing can enhance the nature of inter-
tions between teachers and pupils almost in direct proportion to
e amount of focusing on important aspects of the teaching-learn-
g behavior during playback—as opposed to unfocused general
ewing practices. Obviously, focusing needs to be handled by a
nsitive leader who has an understanding of what took place
uring the teaching situation. This person can call attention to
pects of performance that can be remedied, rather than to ir-
levant and noncorrectable aspects.

An underlying assumpton of CBTE programs is that learning ex-
eriences for teachers-to-be must utilize information about their
rofessional needs, learning styles, and learning rates. On the basis
f such knowledge, university instructors can counsel students to
nter self-directed study; for example, a programed word attack
ook for teachers. Trainees may also engage in classroom projects,
ork with expert teachers in given areas, and analyze new instruc-
onal materials as alternate routes to competency achievement.

One benefit of the personalized approach to learning used in
ewer teacher preparation programs is the internal consistency of
he system. By incorporating principles of diagnosis, individualiza-
on, and flexibility, preservice preparation can provide models of
ood teaching which may be adopted by students. This idea receives
trong support from those who contend that, although at least two

generations of teachers have been aware of the importance of individualization, most continue to instruct children in large groups in much the same way they themselves were taught in elementary schools. Braun (2) comments, "Change in practice will take place only when teachers as students have experienced individualized instruction."

In concluding this discussion of competency based education, despite some strong statements to the contrary, it should be remembered that CBTE does not claim that student acquisition of specific sets of competencies will necessarily result in a new group of master teachers in the schools. It implies, instead, that once such competencies are verified, the original lists will be modified. Furthermore, many educators are in agreement with De Vault, Andersen, and Dickson (3) that even if

> the whole of teaching as an art somehow defies analysis, the systematic planning of many experiences can still be undertaken. . . . The teacher will operate as an individual person with his pupils, but he can be trained in many of the skills and techniques that will facilitate his performance.

COLLEGE B—Composite Model

Type State supported, multipurpose university coeducational

Enrollment 15,000 undergraduates, 5,000 full- and part-time graduates

In the early 1970s, College B initiated a two-year review of its elementary education program. To expedite this undertaking, the staff sought and received some financial support and complete administrative blessings for the proposed study. The reasons behind the proposal were varied: an increasing recognition of the inadequacies of the present form of preparation, a stubborn reluctance to remove the good with the ineffectual portions of its teacher education program, and a high degree of resistance to pressures that threatened to replace reason with faddism.

The following description includes experiences and collective wisdom drawn from a number of colleges as they have worked toward procedural and substantive changes to improve the quality of their programs. Our composite model undertook a rigorous review of its undergraduate courses and practicum offerings by means of three steps:

1. Collaborative efforts involving an interdisciplinary university task force and a consortium of representatives from appropriate groups

2. The design and implementation of a new program resulting from recommendations of the above

3. A plan for the effective evaluation of the new program

Brief descriptions of each step will follow in the next sections of this report.

Collaborative Efforts

TASK FORCE

Convinced that a shared responsibility for teacher preparation is highly desirable, College B engaged in dialogues with members of other departments as an early step toward the improvement of the teacher education program. Shortly after, an interdisciplinary task force began meeting on a weekly basis. The education staff frankly admitted that it did not have the full expertise to develop outstanding teachers; academic department members responded that their responsibilities should not cease with specific course offerings. Consensus indicated that the career development of students was a continuing process. Moreover, everyone expressed concern about what happens educationally and socially in the public schools. They believed that teaching requires such varied sensitivities, information, and skills that only a carefully conceived, interdisciplinary approach can prepare teachers for the schools of today and tomorrow.

One outgrowth of the work of the task force will be mentioned under Program Revision. Another resulted in an integrated course in the area of social services. The group agreed that understandings equally appropriate for teachers, social workers, nurses, medical practitioners, and other students in related fields could be offered more economically and effectively to such individuals by a single department rather than by each of several. Furthermore, it was hoped that those preparing to work in these fields would gain knowledge and respect for their complementary roles.

CONSORTIUM

A second step toward program revision involved the formation of a consortium of representatives from the university, local schools, educational associations, students, and community groups. The consortium posed several searching questions: What is an ideal teacher for today's elementary schools? What knowledge, skills, and attitudes should the teacher possess? What learning activities and experiences will enable prospective teachers to acquire these goals? How can we determine when preservice teachers have attained the goals?

Beginning with a definition of an ideal teacher, the group described in broad terms the teacher as one who makes intelligent decisions about instructional procedures for the great variety of learners with whom he or she works—decisions based upon a sound understanding of learning processes, child development, curriculum, and diagnostic techniques. Participants expressed concern for what the teacher *is* as well as for what the teacher *does*, enumerating qualities that make the teacher humane. The teacher should hold a positive attitude toward human potential and demonstrate respect for the integrity of the individual. The group viewed knowledge and skill as important but placed more emphasis upon the teacher's affective development.

Members of the consortium turned to a number of professional sources as they tried to find answers to their initial questions. They brought to light that little is known for certain about the relationship between teacher performance in the classroom and student growth in reading. The almost universal neglect of the teacher as a critical variable in research on instruction led the committee to voice a strong plea for well-designed studies which would examine all important variables affecting student achievement. By doing so, the group was again expressing the view that teaching is an extremely complex process—one in which an undetermined number of factors interact simultaneously such as administrative policies and teacher morale, individual teacher and student characteristics, classroom organizational patterns, and teacher-peer acceptance of individual pupils.

Following initial discussions, the consortium divided into subgroups to accomplish certain tasks. For example, Subgroup I dealt with selection procedures of teaching candidates at the university and in the schools; Subgroup II looked at problems encountered by inservice teachers; Subgroup III attempted to predict the future of education and its influence upon teacher preparation programs; and so forth. Brief references to their work follow.

Subgroup I. This group embarked upon a study of teacher selection practices at the university level and in the local schools. It ound evidence that academic records and test scores leave much to be desired in judging a student's potential success in college and teaching. It reviewed the education department's screening procedures for entrance to teacher education. Although the department looked closely at the quality of its applicants by studying written statements about their motivations for teaching and their previous experiences related to teaching, the overabundance of teachers in the 1970s prompted the group to recommend additional steps in the selection process. The first involved small group and individual interviews (preferably during the sophomore year, if not earlier) by local school and university personnel. The interview committee, already acquainted with the applicants' academic reports and personal statements, could explore students' interests in some depth and their reasons for choosing to work with children in educational settings. Respondents in turn could inquire about job opportunities, special programs, alternate routes to certification, or other areas of concern.

Subgroup I also proposed the introduction of checkpoints at intervals of student progress. These were for the purpose of exchanging frank comments about progress, program content and activities, current aspirations, and the supply-demand situation. Another proposal was to the effect that only quality candidates be permitted to enroll in teacher preparation. The subgroup presented strong arguments for setting a reasonable quota of entrants until prevailing conditions change.

This same committee recommended that school systems employ higher-level selection procedures in hiring new teachers. Specifically, the group suggested that, when obtainable, personnel committees should require samples of the candidate's actual teaching ability and success. Samples might include videotapes of the candidate as he worked with children, individually and in small groups; lesson plans with comments from the observing supervisor; slides of classroom projects completed with children; impromptu discussions on how the applicant might handle sample school problems; and some indication of how the candidate proposes to keep up-to-date in his field of interest.

Subgroup II. This committee started with the premise that the major problems of preservice education can be understood in relation to the inservice needs of teachers. Obtaining lists of current requests for assistance from the local board of education and the university's department of education, the group ranked areas and topics that appeared troublesome. Additional data were gathered by means of responses from questionnaires address to on-the-job personnel and to former teachers who had left the profession for on reason or another. The group recognized that opinions about preparation programs may not necessarily reflect program effectiveness; therefore, so that a high degree of objectivity could be assured the group exercised great caution in wording items to be rated on a scale of values and those calling for free responses. As a follow up o the questionnaire study, the subgroup interviewed a number o former graduates to obtain further suggestions regarding the improvement of teacher preparation in reading. When information from these sources was compiled and returned to the consortium a a whole, it formed a substantial base from which to derive high priority considerations for changes in teacher education.

Subgroup III. This group was composed of persons with varying backgrounds, from a nuclear physicist to a leader in the local teachers' association. Asked to "dream the impossible dream," the group agreed to take quantum leaps into a future time frame for the purpose of making rational judgments about developments which might have an impact on teacher education. Obviously, it is difficult to establish educational goals for the future when the uncertainties and complexities of living in the present threaten to envelop us so completely as to preclude the future as a dimension of our thinking. Nevertheless, the group followed two routes: 1) they attempted to describe what conditions teachers probably will face in 1990 and 2) they drafted educational goals in keeping with the predictions.

To facilitate their work, the committee solicited position papers about the future written by persons well-informed in several areas of the social sciences. The experts were asked to substantiate their forecasts to help the committee in selecting those that might hold high potential for changes in teacher preparation. From these papers, and from ideas gleaned in the professional literature, the group identified seventy-three possible goals. The goals were submitted to members of the full consortium with whom a Delphi technique was used to produce increasing agreement among the participants and to probe priorities held by the members. Perhaps one example will suffice in this report.

Individualization of instruction has been talked about, of course, since Rousseau's *Emile*, but it appeared to the forecasters hat it could become a reality in the last quarter of the twentieth century. Thus, it may be even more important for educators to consider such variables as children's cognitive styles, reinforcement schedules, reward preferences, and learning modalities. Teachers skilled in offering individualized procedures may be expected to provide such alternatives as computer assisted instruction at home via telephone and television; tutorial sessions with the teacher interspersed with periods of independent study and computerized instruction; or group sessions in scientific inquiry guided by the teacher and, perhaps, a community member who works in the area of scientific investigation.

As individualization of instruction becomes an educational reality, the number of options for prospective teachers (as well as for the nation's children) will augment significantly, requiring changes in staff roles. Futurists predict an increase in teacher aides, paraprofessionals, and community resource people. Open classrooms and team teaching also necessitate greater use of differentiated staffind. Sand (4:238) pictures classrooms that are not unlike libraries and living rooms where appointments and independent learning take place. Sand envisions that the teacher of the future may spend possibly one-third time with pupils and the remainder in preparation and research. The school may be nongraded, decentralized, and broadly based in decision-making which involves children, teachers, parents, and others. Education can, and will, happen anywhere through an unlimited number of activities, if colleges and universities respond to the challenges of preparing teachers who can function effectively in varied settings.

Program Revision

Because today's teacher is a facilitator of learning, a coordinator of activities leading to learning, a discussion leader, and a community participant, the continuing process of preparing teachers requires a liberal education firmly buttressed by the best professional education that colleges can offer. College B's new program emphasizes both the liberal arts and general education of students, but this section will describe primarily the changes in preparation in reading.

From a traditional three credit hour course in Reading Methods and its counterpart in Language Arts, College B restructured the reading component of undergraduate education to include four courses (twelve credit hours): Teaching Word Attack Skills, Language Arts in the Elementary School, Methods and Materials in Elementary School Reading, and Practicum in Diagnostic and Corrective Reading. This dramatic change occurred as a result of the high priority given to reading by the consortium which supported the view that it is impossible for one course to provide the breadth and depth of knowledge expected of prospective teachers who need exposure to the full range of approaches to the teaching of reading and the varying philosophies that undergird them. Previously, students had learned about two or three reading systems, largely through examination of commercial products.

In fairness, it should be noted that College B would be in the vanguard to deny that accumulation of credits in reading per se automatically leads to better teaching. Instead, it would argue that broader knowledge in tandem with earlier, more frequent, and higher quality teaching experiences will strengthen its program. The recent endorsement of the concept that teacher preparation can be effective only to the extent that a substantial portion takes place in the schools is indicative of the serious college attempts to integrate theory and practice in each of its revised courses. Moreover, by early exposure to the realities of teaching, universities can encourage promising candidates, discourage marginal ones, and continue to monitor the commitment of all who enter the profession. Ideally, too, it was felt that frequent contacts with children in classrooms will help neophyte teachers adjust with greater confidence and competence in their initial teaching assignments.

A vital part of the new program involves varied experiences with children in a number of different settings, with the faculty attempting to organize these experiences from relatively simple to complex so that the student's developing skills can be evaluated by the student as well as by the supervisors. Beginning in the sophomore year (whenever possible) and continuing through the final semester, the student takes part in the following learning activities in class, in the field, and in the reading center: 1) those which do not require direct teaching, such as interviews of representatives of the school and community, classroom observations during which the student completes a case study of a child, and attendance at teachers' meetings and planning sessions; and 2) direct involvement with pupils, in college and cluster-school sites, through tutoring, microteaching, instructing small and large groups, working with minority and special education groups, and serving as a teacher aide.

Obviously, placing more and more practicum activities in the field will not correct present deficiencies in teacher education. In the past, criticisms have pointed to field experiences which have been inadequately supervised and unsatisfactorily woven into the total fabric of teacher preparation. The need for higher quality, better supervised experiences, both on the campus and in the field, is still a critical issue. In the 1970s, as the present oversupply of teachers continues, colleges and school districts have unique opportunities to design field assignments, to develop high standards for student-supervisory participation, and to maintain high standards of performance.

During the junior year, students at College B take a fifteen credit block of methods courses—language arts, math, reading, science, and social studies—taught by an interdisciplinary team on campus on Mondays and Wednesdays. In a practicum on Tuesdays and Thursdays, students go to classrooms where they teach activities related to each of the methods courses and assist teachers in other ways. In most cases, students are assigned in teams of two and they are expected to arrange regular planning times with their practicum teachers. Professor teams coordinate the program with students and practicum teachers, observing students and offering inservice education for the teachers.

Following practicum experiences related to the methods block, juniors or seniors enroll in Practicum in Diagnostic and Corrective Reading. The practicum includes observations, assessment and prescription, instruction, and evaluation. In the phase on Assessment and Prescription, for example, students are assigned to classrooms to work with small groups of children. With the help of their supervising teachers, they determine the reading needs of each child in their group and plan appropriate instructional programs. The ten hours devoted to Instruction call for teaching groups of children for whom they have prescribed instructional programs. Throughout the practicum, students keep detailed records of their experiences in logs or journals, including items such as: extent of individualization, basal, supplementary materials and activities, management techniques, and copies of several lesson plans. (See Chapter 2 for other details of this program.)

As seniors, students engage in twelve weeks of student teaching where, because of their previous experiences, they move rapidly into instructional roles. Clusters of students are assigned to field-site schools where cooperating teachers and university professors work with students in planning their work. Frequent observations, weekly seminars, and individual and group conferences take place in these teaching centers. At the conclusion of student teaching, prospective teachers may register for an additional three week placement in another situation, should it be necessary or desired. Anticipated outcomes of the new program for elementary teacher trainees are: 1) graduates should be able to integrate the theory and practice of teaching more effectively, and 2) the close cooperation between school and college staff should generate a dynamic program of high quality.

For many years, College B had recognized that teaching candidates enter the profession with varying cultural, educational, and personal backgrounds. For this reason, the staff willingly recommitted itself to the concept of individual differences when the consortium recommended that the revised program should include a broad range of learning activities. The reading staff, believing that options honor the diversity of talents and needs of students, now provides greater flexibility in its program by offering choices of activities for accomplishing any given outcome. Beyond the usual lectures and recommended professional readings, students are discovering values in small group discussions, workshops focused on topics of special interests and needs, observations of demonstration lessons with children in classrooms, peer teaching, independent study, and simulation experiences which require responses approximating those expected in actual classrooms. Through activities such as these, students find they are becoming more involved in personal routes to learning.

Program Evaluation

The reading staff of College B views evaluation as a continuous, cooperative, and systematic process of determining the quality of its program. Because the staff wants timely information which can be used for program modification purposes, it chose to incorporate both progress and outcome evaluation procedures. Progress or formative evaluation provides data to show whether the program is making gains toward achieving its objectives; it helps decision makers to take corrective action as needed, since it supplies information about student progress during the program's developmental stages. Formative evaluation, then, calls attention to critical points, for example, poor student performance on certain objectives, which

an be investigated immediately. Outcome or summative evalua-
ions take place after the student has completed the semester or
ntire program. It leads to judgments regarding the value of the
rogram, enabling administrators and educators to decide whether
he program should be continued in its present form. Often, when
utcome procedures alone are used in the evaluation process, the re-
ulting delay wastes time, effort, and money. This rationale under-
ies the use of both process and outcome evaluation procedures,
articularly when the former facilitates improvement of an instruc-
ional sequence while it is still amenable to modification.

In its choice of instruments for gathering ongoing program in-
ormation, College B selected the following:

1. Observation forms for use by college and cooperating reading teachers in monitoring prospective teachers' work in
tutorial and classroom settings.

2. Questionnaires to teacher trainees with open-ended questions. Examples: What has been the most valuable part of
this course for you? What kinds of difficulties did you en-
counter? What suggested changes should be made in
course content, learning activities, supervision practices?
(The same questionnaire is sent to all members of the team,
including course instructors, cooperating teachers and
supervisors, and school principals.)

3. Systematic analyses of individual differences among teacher candidates. Gathered from a number of sources, these
data can lead to determining which differences are likely to
make the program more effective for some students than
for others. They include: previous experiences related to
teaching; choices of learning activities, attitudes and
beliefs (self-concept, for example, as evidenced by feelings
that one can learn, can cope with difficulties, can take responsibility); and log books of classroom observations and
participations.

4. Shared intuitions of college and school observers concerning individual differences of prospective teachers that
cannot be appraised otherwise.

5. Teaching samples: video- and audiotaped lessons, classroom projects, lesson plans, and results of interaction
analyses.

6. Small group and individual conferences with students
about the program, their progress in it, and suggested
changes.

Several of these instruments were constructed by members of an evaluation team who found that standardized procedures for measuring important items did not exist.

Lest it be thought that College B is striving too diligently to "shore up" relatively minor aspects of its total program at the expense of global ones, we turn now to the plans for outcome evaluation. Although these are not complete, nor perfected, the college envisions at least two steps: 1) a reexamination of goals for teacher preparation in reading, and 2) a study of graduates of the new program during a one-year internship in a teaching center.

Because concern for the prospective teacher's total growth goes far beyond the usual preoccupations with the acquisition of knowledge and skills, the first procedure will consider the broader, more fundamental objectives of the program. The original goals will be examined in light of divergencies from them during the developmental phases, to determine whether the changes made will lead to valuable additions. When the list is complete, the goal statement will be resubmitted to the consortium for review and confirmation. An evaluation team continues to draft and validate outcome measures for each component of the program. It also is attempting to examine information about possible side effects—unexpected outcomes, both negative and positive—"We don't want teachers to teach children *how* to read but learn to hate reading in the process."

A major part of outcome evaluation will be based upon a one-year intern placement for trainees who graduate from the first three consecutive years of the revised preparation program. In the past colleges and schools have expected fledgings, after accepting positions, to undergo an abrupt metamorphosis equivalent to the emergence of a striking lepidopteron from a cocoon or a beautiful, mature swan from an ugly duckling. Overnight, as it were, graduates were to become fully-qualified teachers. For the hundreds of promising young people who abandoned the field, and for those embittered ones who remained, a transitional year might have helped them become capable professionals. Not unexpectedly, the college decided that lip service to career growth on a continuum with several phases was no longer acceptable; the department of education must extend support and professional expertise until beginning teachers reach higher levels of competence.

The internship concept is not new but College B, realizing the potential of this approach, will implement it in established teacher enters where teams of experienced and novice teachers will work together in new partnership roles with university and school personnel. A college coordinator will be assigned full-time to the teaching center, providing supportive services for teacher teams, helping interns through conferences and seminars, and collecting data for use in evaluating the revised program.

Interns will be paid, although they will begin with a partial teaching load. The remainder of their school day will allow opportunities for experience in diagnostic teaching of a group with reading problems, and participation in planning conferences and seminars. Gradually intern responsibilities will increase to a full teaching schedule.

During the experimental internship program, the college will seek answers to such questions as: After trainee experience in the new program, what type of teaching responsibilities is the trainee ready to assume? On the basis of the training received, what additional responsibilities should a trainee be capable of performing? What preparation is needed to enable the trainee to move along the continuum? Can we reasonably add training in the desired area of advancement to our undergraduate program?

Taking stock during the internship year will serve two functions: the college will have a better picture of the strengths and weaknesses of its offerings, and the student can be helped to grow in ability to identify and remedy his or her teaching deficiencies. Hopefully, the intern will take the initiative to overcome deficits during the transition period. Moreover, the year may provide an excellent opportunity for the young teacher to integrate what may have appeared to be a series of isolated experiences in prebaccalaureate training.

Future Emphases

Throughout this report, and the earlier one, the teacher is viewed as the leader of the movement to improve the teaching of reading in the nation's schools. This is not to say that the teacher alone is responsible for student success. New teaching methodologies, new materials, and new organizational plans will continue to be promoted in the future. Unless the teacher can select wisely and adapt ideas for use with individual children in different settings, little progress can be expected.

The next decade, perhaps more than any in the past, will demonstrate the critical importance of high quality teacher preparation. At present, there is no evidence to thrust all thinking about teacher education in reading in any one direction. Colleges and universities will need to explore a whole range of possible alternatives as they restructure their programs. That teacher education should have a strong knowledge base is a well-established fact. Programs of the future, however, must give more weight to the affective development of teachers as an essential ingredient of teaching and learning.

The new look at teacher education also will recognize the need to include the collaborative efforts of all who will be directly involved in such decisions. Greater emphasis upon field placements will require the development of closer professional relationships with cooperating elementary schools. And codetermination holds high potential for better decision making, because it forces individuals to clarify their thinking as they take time to explain and convince others of their views.

A paramount concern to many educators is the absence of serious research upon which to build better teacher preparation programs. Educational researchers must play a more active role in the future in expanding the number of well-designed studies related to decisions required by teacher educators—a role involving work with appropriate groups to determine the most efficacious means of undertaking such research.

Finally, there is need for reliable and valid evaluation procedures. Colleges and universities are struggling to ascertain whether their programs will make an impact upon improving teacher quality. Until more sophisticated techniques are developed, the generally mediocre ones currently in use merely spotlight this critical condition. Again, professional teamwork could have far-reaching consequences.

These modest proposals are neither new nor startling to those in teacher education. If, however, the focus of activity in the next decade (indeed, the next quarter of a century) is directed toward advancement in the areas of research on topics relevant to teacher education and on devising more discriminating evaluation instruments and plans, the possibilities for improved teacher education programs appear virtually endless.

REFERENCES

1. Austin, Mary C., and others. *The Torch Lighters: Tomorrow's Teachers of Reading.* Cambridge, Massachusetts: Harvard University Press, 1961.

2. Braun, Frederick G. "Individualization: Making It Happen," *Reading Teacher,* 25 (January 1972), 316-318.

3. DeVault, M. Vere, Dan W. Andersen and George E. Dicksen. *Competency Based Teacher Education:* I, "Problems and Prospects for the Decades Ahead." Berkeley, California: McCutchan, 1973, 27.

4. Sand, Ole. "Curriculum Change," *The Curriculum: Retrospect and Prospect,* Seventieth Yearbook of the National Society for the Study of Education, Part I. Chicago, Illinois: University of Chicago Press, 1971, 219-244.

5. Sartain, Harry W., and Paul E. Stanton (Eds.), *Modular Preparation for Teaching Reading.* Newark, Delaware: International Reading Association, 1974.

6. Stieglits, Ezra L., and Robert T. Rude. *Methods and Materials in Teaching Reading: Competency Based Approach* (Second Edition). Providence, Rhode Island: Rhode Island College, 1975.

PARTICIPATING SCHOOLS*

Alabama

> Auburn University
> Florence State University
> Troy State University

Arizona

> Arizona State University at Flagstaff
> Arizona State University at Tempe
> University of Arizona

Arkansas

> Arkansas State University
> State College of Arkansas

California

> California State University at Long Beach
> California State University at Los Angeles
> California State University at Sacramento
> California State University at San Diego
> Loyola University
> San Francisco State
> University of California at Riverside
> University of the Pacific
> University of Southern California at Los Angeles

Colorado

> Colorado College
> Colorado State University at Fort Collins
> University of Colorado at Boulder
> University of Denver

Connecticut

> Central Connecticut State College
> Southern Connecticut State College
> University of Connecticut at Storrs

District of Columbia

> District of Columbia Teachers College
> George Washington University

Florida

> Florida Southern College
> University of Florida at Gainesville
> University of Miami
> University of Tampa

*Nine schools are omitted from this list for lack of identification.

Georgia

University of Georgia at Athens

Hawaii

University of Hawaii at Honolulu

Illinois

Illinois State University at Normal
National College
Southern Illinois University
University of Illinois at Urbana
Western Illinois University

Indiana

Ball State University
Butler University
Indiana State University at Terre Haute
Indiana University at Bloomington
Valparaiso University

Iowa

Maycrest College
University of Iowa at Iowa City
Wartburg College

Kansas

Fort Hays Kansas State College
Kansas State Teachers College at Emporia
University of Kansas at Lawrence
Washburn University of Topeka

Kentucky

Eastern Kentucky University
Morehead State University
Murray State University
Western Kentucky University

Louisiana

Louisiana Technical University
Loyola University of the South
McNeese State College
Northeast Louisiana University
Northwestern State University of Louisiana
Southeastern Louisiana University
University of Southwestern Louisiana

Maryland

Frostburg State College
University of Maryland at College Park

Massachusetts

Boston College
Boston University
Salem State College
State Teachers College at Boston
University of Massachusetts at Amherst
Westfield State College

Michigan

Andrews University
Central Michigan University
Michigan State University at East Lansing
Northern Michigan University
Western Michigan University

Minnesota

Mankato State College
Moorhead State College
University of Minnesota at Minneapolis
Winona State College

Mississippi

Delta State College
Mississippi State University at State College
University of Mississippi at University
University of Southern Mississippi

Missouri

Central Missouri State College
Northeast Missouri State University
St. Louis University
University of Missouri at Columbia

Montana

Eastern Montana College
University of Montana at Missoula

Nebraska

Kearney State College
University of Nebraska at Omaha

New Jersey

Kean College of New Jersey

New York

Adelphia University
City University of New York at Brooklyn
City University of New York at New York City
City University of New York at Queens
Columbia University
New York University at New York
State University College at Buffalo
State University College at Cortland
State University College at New Paltz
State University College at Potsdam
University of Rochester

Ohio

Fenn College
Kent State University
Ohio State University at Columbus
University of Cincinnati
Youngstown State University

Oklahoma

East Central State College
Northwestern State College
Southwestern State College

Oregon

Lewis and Clark College

Pennsylvania

Bloomsburg State College
Clarion State College
Duquesne University
Edinboro State College
Indiana University of Pennsylvania
Millersville State College
Pennsylvania State University at University Park
Shippensburg State College
Temple University
University of Pittsburgh

Rhode Island

Rhode Island College

South Carolina

University of South Carolina at Columbia

South Dakota

> Augustana College
> University of South Dakota at Vermillion

Tennessee

> Austin Peay State University
> Middle Tennessee State University
> University of Tennessee at Knoxville

Texas

> East Texas State University
> Sam Houston State University
> Texas A&M University
> Texas Technological University
> Texas Woman's University
> University of Texas at Austin

Utah

> Brigham Young University

Vermont

> University of Vermont at Burlington

Virginia

> College of William and Mary
> Madison College
> University of Virginia at Charlottesville

Washington

> Eastern Washington State College
> Washington State University at Pullman
> Western Washington State College

West Virginia

> Marshall University
> Morris Harvey College

Wisconsin

> Cardinal Stritch College
> Marquette University
> University of Wisconsin at La Crosse
> University of Wisconsin at Madison
> University of Wisconsin at Milwaukee
> University of Wisconsin at Platteville
> University of Wisconsin at River Falls
> University of Wisconsin at Superior
> University of Wisconsin at Whitewater

Appendix A

STUDY PROCEDURES

The general plan of the follow up study included: 1) the gathering of data from a large number of colleges to ascertain the current status of the recommendations made in *The Torch Lighters*, respondents' reactions to changes that had recently taken place in their teacher preparation programs, and their recommendations for the improvement of future programs; and 2) a collection of detailed descriptions of reading programs from a selected group of respondents.

The 74 colleges and universities that participated in the field study of *The Torch Lighters* formed the nucleus of the second study. A supplementary number of colleges and universitites then had to be selected to augment the 74. Unfortunately, the names of all the colleges and universities that participated in the first study were no longer available. Therefore, all teacher preparatory schools included in the International Reading Association publication, *Graduate Programs and Faculty in Reading*, were contacted. In all, questionnaires were sent to 200 schools; returns were received from 161, or 73.2 percent.

In analyzing the 161 responses it was apparent that many of the replies reported in part 2 of the questionnaire (recent changes in preparatory programs) represented a departure from the predominant programs for the preparation of prospective teachers of reading. As a result, 50 colleges and universities were asked to participate more fully in the study either by submitting more detailed descriptions of their programs or by participating in a follow up field interview. Results of this part of the study are reported in Chapters 2 and 4.

Tabulation of the questionnaire

Several problems arose in the tabulation of the results. For instance, the comments that accompanied some of the checked columns did not always support one another or sometimes represented a contradiction. Fortunately, these deviations were infrequent and when they did occur the checked column of the respondent was accepted.

Probably a greater tabulation difficulty could be attributed to an ambiguity inherent within the questionnaire itself. For example, respondents were given the option of checking column two "to indicate that a modified or stronger version of the recommendation is in effect as specified in the accompanying space for comments." The accompanying comments indicated that in certain cases the changes cited did, in fact, supercede our recommendation; whereas, in other instances the recommendation, while modified, was not in effect as recommended.

One different reporting problem: Four of the recommendations (11, 12, 15, 20) had two or more internal parts. In most instances, the respondents treated the recommendation globally (one check), whereas others treated the component parts of the recommendation individually (multiple checkmarks). The data were treated in two ways. A composite percentage was arrived at for each part of the recommendation by applying the same checkmark to all parts of the recommendation (when only one was provided) and combining these tallies with those supplied by respondents using multiple checkmarks. Results of this nature are reported in Chapter 1. In Appendix C a separation of the two kinds of replies is given.

The first questionnaire was mailed in Spring 1974. The request for more detailed information was made in January 1975, and field visits were made in 1975 and 1976.

RESPONSES TO RECOMMENDATIONS 11, 12, 15 AND 20 WHEN RESULTS ARE NOT TREATED AS A COMPOSITE SCORE.

RECOMMENDATION 11

	N	%	N	%	N	%	N	%	N	%
			Part A		Part B		Part C		Part D	
1. in effect	64	70.3	34	48.6	34	48.6	42	60.0	29	41.4
2. modified or strengthened	20	22.0	24	34.3	21	30.0	20	28.6	15	21.4
3. not in effect	4	4.4	10	14.3	10	14.3	6	8.6	20	28.6
4. not applicable	3	3.3	2	2.9	4	5.7	1	1.4	4	5.7
5. no response	0	0.0	0	0.0	1	1.4	1	1.4	2	2.9
	91	100.0	70	100.1	70	100.0	70	100.0	70	100.0

RECOMMENDATION 12

	N	%	Part A N	Part A %	Part B N	Part B %
in effect	85	58.6	1	6.3	14	87.5
modified or strengthened	36	24.8	3	18.8	2	12.5
not in effect	22	15.2	11	68.8	0	0.0
not applicable	2	1.4	1	6.3	0	0.0
no response	0	0.0	0	0.0	0	0.0
	145	100.0	16	100.2	16	100.0

RECOMMENDATION 15

	N	%	Part A N	Part A %	Part B N	Part B %	Part C N	Part C %	Part D N	Part D %
1. in effect	19	17.1	16	32.0	6	12.0	17	34.0	23	46.0
2. modified or strengthened	14	12.6	10	20.0	4	8.0	11	22.0	10	20.0
3. not in effect	60	54.1	17	34.0	33	66.0	17	34.0	13	26.0
4. not applicable	16	14.4	4	8.0	7	14.0	4	8.0	3	6.0
5. no response	2	1.8	3	6.0	0	0.0	1	2.0	1	2.0
	111	100.0	50	100.0	50	100.0	50	100.0	50	100.0

RECOMMENDATION 20

	N	%	Part A N	Part A %	Part B N	Part B %
1. in effect	38	26.4	1	5.9	11	64.7
2. modified or strengthened	24	16.7	3	17.6	5	29.4
3. not in effect	69	48.0	11	64.7	1	5.9
4. not applicable	12	8.3	2	11.7	0	0.0
5. no response	1	0.7	0	0.0	0	0.0
	144	100.1	17	99.9	17	100.0

THE TORCH LIGHTERS REVISITED

A Questionnaire in Three Parts

Part 1 Seeks to determine the utility of the original twenty-two recom mendations made in *The Torch Lighters*

Part 2 Seeks to determine significant changes that have taken place at you college in relation to the undergraduate preparation of prospecti teachers of reading

Part 3 Seeks suggested recommendations for the future

Part 1

Following are the twenty-two recommendations published in *The Torc Lighters*. In the corresponding right hand columns would you please chec one or more of the appropriate responses, using the following key:

Check column 1 to indicate that the recommendation is in effect to a sul stantial extent.

Check column 2 to indicate that a modified (or stronger) version of th recommendation is in effect, as specified in the a companying space for comments.

Check column 3 to indicate that the recommendation is not in effect to substantial extent, nor is a modified version in effect.

Check column 4 to indicate that the recommendation is not applicable, specified in the accompanying space for comments.

Recommendations

	1	2	3	4
1. That all students be required to make formal application to teacher education programs at the end of the sophomore year—selection criteria to include degree of academic proficiency, mental and emotional maturity, indication of aptitude for teaching, and competency in the elementary grade skills.				
Comments:				
2. That students be permitted (if not encouraged) to elect a field of concentration other than elementary education, provided basic requirements in the education program are met, including the equivalent of a three semester hour course in the teaching of reading and one course in student teaching.				
Comments:				

	1	2	3	4
That those faculty members charged with the responsibility for training prospective teachers make every effort to inculcate in their students a sense of pride in their chosen profession.				
Comments:				
That senior faculty members, prominent in the field of reading, play a more active role in the instruction of undergraduates and assume responsibility for teaching at least one undergraduate course.				
Comments:				
That the class time devoted to reading instruction, whether taught as a separate course or integrated with the language arts, be equivalent to at least three semester hours of credit.				
Comments:				
That the basic reading instruction offered to prospective elementary teachers be broadened to include content and instructional techniques appropriate for the intermediate and upper grades.				
Comments:				
That college instructors continue to emphasize that no one method of word recognition, such as phonic analysis, be used to the exclusion of other word attack techniques. That students be exposed to a variety of opinions related to other significant issues of reading, such as grouping policies, prereading materials, techniques of beginning reading instruction, and teaching machines.				
Comments:				
8. That college instructors take greater responsibility in making certain that their students have mastered the principles of phonic and structural analysis.				
Comments:				

	1	2	3	4

9. That a course in basic reading instruction be required of all prospective secondary school teachers.

Comments:

10. That colleges offer a course, or inservice training, in reading instruction specifically designed for principals, supervisors, and cooperating teachers.

Comments:

11. a) That more use be made of the case study or problem centered approach so that students are given the opportunity to relate theory to a particular problem and ultimately to analyze, interpret, and solve the problem.
    b) That tape recording and films of classroom activities be utilized to supplement course offerings.
    c) That students be provided with directed observational experiences in local schools concurrently with their course work in reading, or that they have the opportunity of observing classroom teaching on closed circuit television.
    d) That college administrators make every effort to coordinate reading instruction with the practice teaching program.

Comments:

12. That all prospective teachers become acquainted with techniques, interpretation, and evaluation of current and past research.

That all prospective teachers be introduced to professional reading journals.

Comments:

13. That the staff responsible for teaching reading and/or language arts courses be sufficiently augmented to allow each instructor time in which to observe and confer with students during the practice teaching experience and to consult with the cooperating teacher and administrative personnel.

Comments:

	1	2	3	4

4. That additional experimental research be initiated in the areas of critical reading, study skills, and grouping practices.

Comments:

5. a) That the colleges recruit, train, and certify cooperating teachers.
   b) That cooperating teachers, after training and college certification, serve in the capacity of associates to the college.
   c) That as associates to the college, cooperating teachers participate in the formulation of practice teaching programs, in related seminars and in the final evaluation of student performance.
   d) That as associates to the college, cooperating teachers receive financial remuneration commensurate with their roles.

Comments:

6. That colleges appoint a liaison person to work directly with the local school system to achieve closer cooperation between the schools and the college and to assist the public schools in upgrading reading and other academic instruction.

Comments:

7. That colleges encourage students to remain in local cooperating schools for a full day during the practice teaching program so that their understanding of the continuity of the reading program may be strengthened.

Comments:

8. That not more than two students be assigned to practice teach simultaneously in one cooperating classroom.

Comments:

9. That where students are assigned to one classroom during practice teaching, provisions be made for them to participate in directed observation programs at other grade levels.

Comments:

	1	2	3	4

20. That where the student is found to have specific weaknesses in understanding the total reading program, the student be required to return to the college, following practice teaching, for additional course work.

That where a student is weak in the area of instructional techniques, student apprenticeship be prolonged until a predetermined degree of competency is attained.

Comments:

21. That colleges reexamine the criteria used to evaluate students during the practice teaching experience to ensure that a passing grade in practice teaching does, in fact, mean that the student has achieved the desired level of competency in teaching reading and other elementary grade skills.

Comments:

22. That colleges establish a program to follow up their graduates with a view toward determining to what extent preparation has been adequate and what weaknesses, if any, exist in student training.

Comments:

Part 2

Would you please indicate below those changes in your college program that have taken place in recent years which have affected the undergraduate preparation of prospective teachers of reading.

Year   Nature of the Change   Evaluation

Part 3

Would you please indicate below any recommendations you would make improve present or future baccalaureate programs for the preparation teachers of reading.

Thank You For Your Cooperation

Name of respondent _____

Mailing address _____

_____

Cover design by Philip Blank

J/D2777.....